80 Years of
Civil Aviation

80 Years of
Civil Aviation

Leo Marriott

SUNBURST BOOKS

This edition first published
in 1997 by
Sunburst Books,
Kiln House,
210 New Kings Road,
London SW6 4NZ.

© Sunburst Books 1997

ISBN 1 85778 279 8

Acknowledgements
Leo Marriott wrote the text.
Simon Forty wrote the captions.
Anthony Wirkus did the photo
research and design.
Austin Brown took the photographs
except for these:
via Leo Marriott p8, 11, 12, 15,
16, 20, 21, 28, 30, 33, 57, 66,
67, 68, 69(top), 81(top),
205(top), 214, 215, 216, 217,
218, 219, 220/221.
Boeing p63, 222, 223, 224.

Printed and bound in China

PAGE 1: Aer Lingus DH84 Dragon
EI-ABI Iolar *seen at Bristol.*

PREVIOUS PAGE: *Boeing 767-
3P6ER A40-GR Rastaq is leased by
Gulf Air from Polaris.*

RIGHT: *Thai Air 747-207B HS-TGF
was delivered on 11 September
1980 and is seen nine years later.*

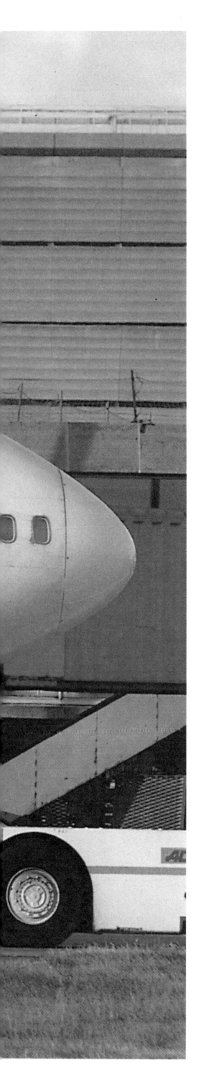

Contents

First Flight Chronology

17 December 1903
Wilbur and Orville Wright's
first flight at Kittyhawk

1919 de Havilland DH4A
Vickers Vimy Commercial
Handley Page O/7
Westland Limousine
Blériot Spas 27
Junkers F13
de Havilland DH16

1920 de Havilland DH18
Fokker FII
Handley Page O/10

1921 Fokker FIII

1922 de Havilland DH34
Handley Page W8b

1923 Farman F60 Goliath

1924 Fokker FVII
Junkers W33

1925 Junkers W10
Fokker FVIIa-3m
Boeing Model 40
Tupolev ANT-3

1926 de Havilland DH66 Hercules
Ford 4-AT

1927 Fokker FX
Armstrong Whitworth Argosy
Lockheed Vega

1928 Leo 213
Boeing Model 80
Short Calcutta

1929 Junkers G38
Curtiss Condor
Airship R101
Dornier X
Fokker FXI
Fokker FXXXII

1930 Junkers Ju52
Boeing Model 200
Northrop Alpha

1931 Handley Page HP42
Lockheed Orion
Fokker FXII

1932 de Havilland DH84 Dragon

1933 Fokker FXX
Boeing Model 247
Douglas DC-2
Northrop Delta

1934 de Havilland DH86 Express
de Havilland DH89 Dragon
Rapide
Fokker FXXXVI
Douglas DC-2
Sikorsky S42
Lockheed L10 Electra
Junkers Ju86

1935 Douglas DC-3
Martin M-130
de Havilland DH90 Dragonfly

1936 Short 'Empire' class

1937 de Havilland DH91 Albatross
Junkers Ju90
Lockheed Model 14 Super Electra
Focke-Wulf Fw200 Condor

1938 Bloch 220
Boeing Model 307 Stratoliner
Boeing Model 314 Clipper
Armstrong Whitworth AW27
Ensign
Douglas DC-4E
de Havilland DH95 Flamingo

1939 Bloch MB161

1940 Lockheed L18 Lodestar

Curtiss C-46 Commando

1942 Douglas DC-4 (C-54 Skymaster)
Avro 685 York

1943 Lockheed Constellation (C-69)

1945 Avro Tudor
Handley Page Hermes
de Havilland DH104 Dove
Vickers Viking
Bristol 170 Freighter
SE161 Languedoc

1946 Douglas DC-6
Ilyushin Il-12
Handley Page Halton
Short Solent
Short Sandringham

1947 Boeing Model 377 Stratocruiser
Convair 240
Martin 2-0-2
Airspeed Ambassador
Antonov An-2

1948 Vickers Viscount

1949 Bristol Brabazon
de Havilland DH106 Comet
Breguet Br763 Provence
Breguet Br761 Deux Ponts

1950 Lockheed L1049 Super
Constellation
de Havilland DH114 Heron

1951 Convair 340
Martin 4-0-4

1952 Bristol Britannia

1953 Douglas DC-7

1954 Boeing 707
Lockheed C-130

1955 Tupolev Tu-104
Sud Ouest Caravelle
Fokker F27 Friendship
Handley Page Herald
Convair 440 Metropolitan

1956 Lockheed L1649A Starliner

1957 Tupolev Tu-114
Lockheed L188 Electra
Ilyushin Il-18
Antonov An-10/An-12

1958 Douglas DC-8
Grumman Gulfstream
North American Sabreliner

1959 Boeing 720
Convair 880
Vickers Vanguard

1960 Hawker Siddeley HS748
Antonov An-24
Convair 580
Canadair CL-44

1961 Convair 990

1962 Vickers VC-10
de Havilland DH121 Trident
Tupolev Tu-134
Aero Spacelines Guppy
NAMC YS-11
Nord Aviation Nord 262

1963 Ilyushin Il-62
Boeing 727
BAC 1-11
Dassault Falcon 20
Learjet 23

1964 Vickers Super VC-10
Shorts Belfast

1965 Douglas DC-9
de Havilland Canada DHC-6 Twin
Otter
Beech 99 Airliner
Britten-Norman BN-2 Islander

1966 Yakovlev YAK-40

1967 Boeing 737
BAC Jetstream
Fokker F28 Fellowship

1968 Tupolev Tu-154
BAC/Aérospatiale Concorde
Tupolev Tu-144

1969 Boeing 747
Let L-410 Turbolet
Fairchild Metro III
Antonov An-28
Cessna Citation

1970 Douglas DC-10
Lockheed L1011 TriStar
Swearingen Metro
Britten-Norman Trislander

1971 Dassault Breguet Mercure
VFW-614
Ilyushin Il-76
CASA C-212 Aviocar

1972 Airbus A300

1974 Shorts 330

1975 de Havilland Canada DHC-7
Dash 7
Yakovlev YAK-42

1976 Ilyushin Il-86
Dassault Falcon 50

1977 EMBRAER EMB-110 Bandeirante

1978 Beechcraft 400
Canadair Challenger

1979 MD-80

1981 Shorts 360
Boeing 767
MD-82
BAe146
Dornier Do228

1982 Airbus A310
Antonov An-124 Ruslan
BAe ATP
Boeing 757
Beech 1900

1983 EMBRAER EMB-120 Brasilia
Saab 340
de Havilland Canada DHC-8
Dash 8

1984 MD-83
ATR42

1985 Fokker 50

1986 Fokker 100

1987 Airbus A320

1988 Boeing 747-400
Ilyushin Il-96
ATR72
Let L-610
Antonov An-225 Mriya

1989 Tupolev Tu-204
McDonnell Douglas MD-90

1990 McDonnell Douglas MD-11
Dassault Falcon 2000

1991 Canadair RJ
Dornier Do328
Airbus A340
BAe Jetsream 41

1992 Airbus A330
Saab 2000

1993 Fokker 70

1994 Boeing 777

1995 EMBRAER EMB-145

*RIGHT: L1649A Starliner N974R
of Maine Coast Airlines at Fort
Lauderdale, 1988.*

80 Years of Civil Aviation:
the History

1919 -1939

'Good morning ladies and gentlemen. On behalf of the captain and crew, we would like to welcome you aboard this flight to New York. Our flight time will be approximately seven hours and we will be cruising at an altitude of 37,000ft. During the flight we will be serving hot meals and a bar service is available. Personal entertainment systems are available at your seat. We hope you will enjoy your flight!'

Every single day thousands of similar announcements are made to the numerous passengers who fly all over the globe at speeds and altitudes undreamt of by the pioneering airmen at the beginning of this century, and in a degree of comfort which compares favourably with anything they might experience on the ground. And yet it is less than 100 years since the Wright brothers first sustained and controlled manned powered flight in December 1903, and only 80 years since regular air services were hesitantly begun in the aftermath of World War 1. In fact commercial air services had made a tentative start even before the war began. The world's first airline was the *Deutsche Luftschiffahrts Aktiengesellschaft* (German Airship Transportation Company), otherwise known as DELAG, which was formed in 1909 with the intention of operating services between German cities using the new Zeppelin airships; flights duly began in November of the following year.

Regular commercial flights with aeroplanes were slower to start, although an aircraft was designed which might well have become the world's first four-engined airliner but for the outbreak of war: the *Bolshoi Baltiskii* (Great Baltic) cabin biplane designed by Igor Sikorsky. It successfully flew first in May 1913. In the following year the magnificent *Ilya Muromets II* demonstrated the potential of the aeroplane by carrying a dozen passengers in stages on a 1,600-mile return journey from St Petersburg to Kiev and back. By comparison, the American air transport industry made a faltering start: the world's first commercial scheduled airline service began on 1 January 1914, flown by the awkwardly named St Petersburg/Tampa Airboat Line between the eponymous towns using a Benoist two-seat flying boat. This did not prosper and flights ceased only four months later. In Britain, the first regular air services were even less ambitious, with Harold Blackburn flying a small biplane of his own design in July 1914 between the neighbouring towns of Leeds and Bradford. Within a few months the world was plunged into a desperate and brutal war, and civil flying was all but forgotten. It was within the crucible of war that the aeroplane would evolve to meet the insatiable demands of the world's military and naval forces.

It was not until the coming of peace at the end of 1918 that thoughts began again to turn to the peaceful uses of aviation and the first real airlines began to operate. In Britain it was Aircraft Transport and Travel which began flying regular services from London to Paris on 25 August 1919, to be followed just over a week later by Handley Page Transport, also on

DH4A of Aircraft Transport and Travel at Hounslow in August 1919. Capt Jerry Shaw of AT&T had flown the first charter on 15 July 1919 from Hendon. The passenger, a Col W. N. Pilkington of Pilkington Glass, needed to get to Paris quickly — it took him nearly three hours to reach Le Bourget. The first scheduled international flight from London took place on 25 August when E. H. Lawford flew a DH4A from Hounslow to Le Bourget. The DH4A could carry two passengers — seated face to face in a cabin in the rear fuselage. It had a top speed of about 120mph and a range of 250 miles.

the same route. The aircraft used by these and other airlines of the period were all converted wartime bombers, a scenario which was to be repeated 25 years later after World War 2. In 1919 the predominant types were the single-engined de Havilland 4A which could carry two passengers in a small cabin occupying the space vacated by the gunner, and the twin-engined Handley Page O/400. Initially the O/400 could carry up to 10 passengers in rather primitive seating; the O/7 version was a more substantial conversion and could carry up to 14 passengers in a proper cabin. Powered by either Rolls-Royce Eagle, Bristol Jupiter or Napier Lion engines, the O/400 had a maximum speed of only 85kts and cruised at considerably less. Although lumbering antiques to modern eyes, the O/400s played their part in establishing the notion of regular air services to the Continent and in fact some of the 43 conversions were the first aircraft to be fitted with the new Marconi radio telephone equipment. Another bomber which had a new life in airliner form was the famous Vickers Vimy – in 1919 the first aircraft to fly the Atlantic successfully, piloted by Alcock and Brown. For airline use the basic twin-engined bomber design was altered by the addition of a bulbous fuselage which had seating for 10 passengers; it was known as the Vimy Commercial. Curiously, no fewer than 40 such aircraft were built for China and were delivered and assembled in 1920, following a number of Handley Page O/400s already in service in the Far East. The first Vimy Commercial for British use was delivered to S. Instone and Co Ltd (later Instone Airlines, one of the airlines which amalgamated to form Imperial Airways in 1924) and flew for many years on services to Paris, Brussels and Cologne.

However everyone involved realised that converted bombers were never going to provide the levels of safety and comfort which passengers were beginning to demand (it should be remembered that flying in those days was the province of the rich and powerful) and all manufacturers began to produce aircraft designed from the start as commercial airliners. One of the first of this new breed was the Westland Limousine, which first flew in 1919. This was a single-engined biplane with a comfortable cabin for up to six passengers between the wings. Although it was the winner of an Air Ministry prize for a design suitable for European services, it actually saw little airline use. On the other hand, de Havilland built on its success with converted DH4 and DH9 bombers and produced a number of new types including the eight-seater DH18 in 1920 and the DH34 which carried a crew of two pilots together with nine passengers in 1922. These were all single-engined cabin biplanes but by 1926 de Havilland had produced the three-engined DH66 Hercules in response to an Imperial Airways specification for an aircraft suitable to carry passengers and mail on routes across the deserts of the Middle East. With a crew of three it cruised at around 95kts, carrying seven passengers and a significant load of cargo or mail. Take-off weight was around 15,600lb.

In the meantime, Handley Page had also moved away from converted bombers and produced the W8, which first flew in twin-engined form in 1919 and could carry up to 15 passengers. This was followed by the W8b in 1922 which, for safety reasons, was limited to carrying 12 passengers. A few examples were flown by Handley Page Transport Ltd and later absorbed into the Imperial Airways' fleet, while several went to the Belgian airline, Sabena. Further development led to the W8e and W9, which had an additional nose-mounted engine, and finally to the W10 of 1925 which reverted to the twin-engined layout, being powered by 450hp Napier Lions. The W10 could seat up to 16 passengers and four were delivered to Imperial Airways. Cruising speed was still well under 100kts and maximum range was in the order of 400 miles.

When Imperial Airways was formed in 1924, it inherited a mixed bag of aircraft; it determined that – for safety reasons – all future aircraft would be multi-engined. Apart from the Handley Page and de Havilland products, it also ordered a new three-engined 20-seater from Armstrong Whitworth. This was the Argosy which first flew in 1926 and started services to Paris in August of that year. It was much larger than its predecessors (maximum all-up weight was 19,200lb) and offered a much improved standard of comfort. Indeed, in 1927 it inaugurated the world's first luxury service – known as the Silver Wing, featuring the then unheard of facility of an in-flight bar manned by a uniformed steward together with a buffet meal. Only seven Argosys were built but they served until 1935, proving popular with passengers, and flew to Paris, Basle, Brussels and Cologne as well as a short period on routes in Africa. In 1931, Imperial Airways was able to introduce the Handley Page HP42 into service on the Paris route for proving trials and thereafter a fleet of eight of these aircraft saw extensive service on European and Middle East routes. With a maximum weight of 29,500lb, the HP42 could carry up to 38 passengers on European flights and was the first four-engined airliner in the world to enter regular service. It also had an all-metal primary structure and most of the fuselage was clad in duralumin plating, although the rest of the fuselage and all the flying surfaces were fabric-covered. The HP42s proved safe and reliable, one aircraft alone flying 1,318,990 miles and carrying no fewer than 160,000 passengers during its career of just over eight years. However, cruising speed was still abysmally slow and by the 1930s significant technical developments were taking place which rendered them obsolete.

The rival Armstrong Whitworth company produced a four-engined monoplane – the Atalanta – in 1932 and eight were ordered for Imperial Airways. With an all-up weight of 21,000lb, this aircraft could carry nine passengers in a luxurious saloon together with a cargo of mail at a cruising speed of 113kts, although range was limited to around 400 miles: not a startling advance, but a step in the right direction. Armstrong Whitworth's next airliner, however, was a significant advance and was perhaps the most impressive of the British pre-WW2 airliners to see any substantial service. This was the AW27 Ensign, a large four-engined monoplane with a high-mounted wing and a traditional tailwheel undercarriage. Take-off weight leapt to 55,000lb and, powered by four 850hp Armstrong Siddeley Tiger engines, it had a range of 800 miles and cruised at 148kts. A later version had more powerful Wright Cyclone radials from America and had a much improved performance with a cruising speed of 156kts and a maximum range of 1,370 miles. Fourteen Ensigns were built and after entering airline service in 1938, several saw arduous war service with BOAC until 1945 when they were flown back to Britain and scrapped.

De Havilland also continued to produce airliners and became best known for its range of small twin-engined aircraft based on the DH84 Dragon biplane which first flew in 1932 powered by 130hp de Havilland Gipsy Major engines. Carrying six passengers, this aircraft was economic to operate and enabled many small airlines to establish viable services in and around the United Kingdom. Operators included Hillmans Airways, Jersey Airways, Aberdeen Airways, and Western Airways. 115 Dragons were built, many for export, and a military version was also produced in Australia. In 1934 de Havilland flew the four-engined DH86 which could carry up to 10 passengers; it was bought by Imperial Airways as well as several other British and overseas airlines. Some 63 examples were produced. However perhaps the most famous aircraft of the period from the de Havilland stable was the DH89 Dragon Rapide which, based on the earlier Dragon, was powered by two 200hp Gypsy Queen engines and could carry up to eight passengers. This handsome looking aircraft, with its fixed undercarriage faired in by streamlined spats that blended into the engine nacelles, was an outstanding success and no fewer than 728 were produced (including wartime military variants) between 1934 and 1944. Several survived to fly with BEA after World War 2 and were not retired until the mid-1960s.

Despite the success of these biplanes, de Havilland also developed more modern designs of which the beautiful DH91 Albatross is probably the best remembered, although only 13 examples were built. Making its first flight in May 1937, the Albatross was powered by four 525hp Gypsy Twelve engines encased in beautifully streamlined nacelles. It was built in two versions, one a specialised long-range mail carrier, and the other a 22-seater high speed passenger airliner. Both cruised at around 180kts but the mailplane had the higher gross weight and an extreme range of 3,300 miles compared to the 1,040 miles of the passenger version.

Unlike most aircraft of the period, the Albatross was of all-wood construction, a technique which was later used to good effect in building the famous Mosquito. de Havilland's other prewar airliner was the all-metal Flamingo which had many other modern features, including a retractable undercarriage, variable pitch propellers and trailing-edge split flaps to improve airfield performance. It took to the air at the end of 1938 but by the time it was ready for airline service Britain was on the brink of war and its subsequent career was mainly as a military transport.

Elsewhere in Europe the outstanding name in the 20 years between the two world wars was that of Antony Fokker, whose fighters produced for the German Army had been the scourge of the allies in the dogfights above the trenches. After the armistice in 1918 he returned to his native Holland and bent his talents to producing civil aircraft. His first successful offering was the Fokker FII of 1920, a single-engined high-wing monoplane carrying four passengers in an enclosed cabin. Approximately 30 were built and used by KLM and some German airlines. However his most significant design, and one of the great milestones in the history of the airliner, was the Fokker FVII which took to the air in April 1924. This was a strong rugged machine carrying seven passengers and powered by a single 360hp Rolls-Royce Eagle engine. Its unique feature, in an era when the biplane reigned supreme, was the high-mounted cantilever wing which required no external bracing thus saving weight and reducing drag. The original FVII completed a spectacular proving flight from the Netherlands to Indonesia and, as a result, was ordered by KLM and other operators. In 1925 Fokker redesigned the aircraft to carry two additional engines, one under each wing, and the resulting tri-motor was known as the FVIIa-3m. In this form the Fokker achieved a runaway success in the United States when it won the Ford Trophy in 1925 in a competition to demonstrate the reliability of various contemporary aircraft. As a result a US production line was set up. The aircraft underwent a substantial development during its subsequent career, being powered by a variety of engines ranging from the original 200hp Wright J4 Whirlwinds to 300hp Pratt & Whitney Wasp Juniors. Over 250 of all versions were produced and customers from all over the world included Pan American, Balair, Japan Air Transport, KLM, Sabena and Western Canada Airways (to name but a few). It was produced under licence in Czechoslovakia, Britain, the United States, Italy and Belgium and was the first truly inter-

First of a long line of Fokker airliners was the FII which was test-flown in October 1919. It carried five passengers – four in a comfortable enclosed cabin and another in the cockpit. It entered service with KLM – which bought two aircraft – in September 1920. It had a top speed of 93mph and a range of nearly 750 miles and would see service into the 1930s.

One of the milestones of civil aviation – the Fokker FVII. Originally powered by a single Rolls-Royce Eagle, the transformation took place with the addition of two outer engines in the FVIIa-3m. It gained immediate recognition in the 1925 Ford Reliability Contest and was to feature prominently in long-range flights for the rest of the decade. In 1926 Floyd Bennett and Richard Byrd flew to the North Pole in a ski-equipped FVIIa-3m. In 1928 a FVIIb-3m powered by three 200hp Wright Whirlwind radial engines was sold to Sir Charles Kingsford Smith. He called his aircraft Southern Cross and in 1928 flew from Oakland, California to Brisbane, Australia, stopping only twice. The c7,500-mile journey took him 83hr 11min. The airliner version was widely built under licence, could seat up to 10 passengers, had a maximum speed of nearly 130mph and a range of about 750 miles. This photograph shows a FVIIb-3m as delivered to the French operator Air Orient.

national airliner. Fokker VII tri-motors made many spectacular pioneering flights, including that of Rear Admiral Byrd to the North Pole in 1926 (the first aircraft ever to land there) and Kingsford Smith's first trans-Pacific flight in 1928.

Fokker went on to develop the high-wing tri-motor formula as the 12/14-seater FX of 1927, the 16-seat FXII of 1933 and, ultimately, the FXX of 1933 which was the first Fokker aircraft with a retractable undercarriage. His last major airliner produced before 1939 was the four-engined FXXXVI which flew in 1934 and could seat up to 32 passengers. However its fabric-covered steel-framed structure was already obsolescent and a fixed undercarriage did nothing for its performance. By now, with war looming, Fokker turned his attention to designing and producing military aircraft and left the production of world beating commercial aircraft to the Americans.

French industry also produced many interesting designs which ranged from the Blériot Spad 27 of 1919, which carried only two passengers, to the magnificent Farman F60 Goliath of 1923 and the famous Leo 213 twin-engined 18-passenger biplane which first flew in 1928. In typical Gallic style, one version of this aircraft was converted to include a 12-seater restaurant as French and British airlines fought to provide the most luxurious service on the prestigious London-Paris route. Today's passengers squashed into a modern jet with short-range high-density seating are perhaps missing something! The level reached by France in the immediate pre-1939 era is best illustrated by the Bloch 220 twin-engined all-metal 16-seater powered by two 985hp Gnome Rhône 14Ns, which entered service with Air France in 1938. Also from the Bloch stable was the MB161 four-engined 33-seater which flew in 1939 and was subsequently resurrected in 1945 as the Sud Est 161 Languedoc.

In Germany, the Junkers concern was pre-eminent in the production of civil airliners, making a tremendous start in 1919 when the prototype F13 took to the air, the world's first all-metal airliner. Powered by a single 160hp Mercedes DIIIa engine, it had a crew of two, carried four passengers and remained in production until 1932 by which time 322 had been built. Of course the design was continually refined, with virtually every suitable available aero engine of German, French, British or American origin being fitted. An enlarged tri-motor version (à la Fokker FVII) was first flown in 1924 and was known variously as the G23 or G24 while a single radial-engined version was known as the W33 or W34. Including military versions, a total of 1,791 of these was built. The most spectacular creation from Junkers was the enormous G38 four-engined monoplane which took to the air in 1929. For its day, it was the Boeing 747 of the age, with a wingspan of 144ft and a gross weight of 52,910lb. Only two were built and both were eventually powered by four 750hp Jumo 204 engines. A total of 34 passengers plus seven crew could be carried, a unique feature of the accommodation being two small cabins situated in the wing leading edges, each seating three passengers who had a fantastic field of view downwards and ahead. Competition for these seats must have been intense! The wing itself was massive in relation to the fuselage but the G38s only cruised at 98kts although their range was just over 2,000 miles.

The most famous design to appear from the Junkers factory was the Junkers Ju52/3m, which closely emulated the career of the earlier Fokker FVII in that both were originally designed as single-engined aircraft. Only six Ju52s were built in this configuration; the seventh production aircraft, which flew in 1931, was powered by three licence-built 575hp Pratt & Whitney Hornets and could carry up to 17 passengers. Later versions were powered by a a variety of other engines. Despite its crude appearance, heightened by its fixed undercarriage and corrugated metal skinning (a Junkers trademark), the Ju52 was a tough old bird which proved extremely adaptable. Not only was it used by airlines all over the world, including the original prewar British Airways, but it was also adapted as a military transport and even used as a bomber in the Spanish Civil War. By 1939 some 2,500 had been built and an equal number was produced during World War 2. After 1945, another 400 were built under licence in France while Spain produced 170. These figures made the Ju52 the second most numerous airliner ever built, only exceeded by the legendary DC-3.

Other German designs prior to the outbreak of war included the Junkers Ju90 and the sleek Focke Wulf Fw200 Condor. The former flew in 1937 and could carry up to 40 passengers but was not ready for airline service by the time war broke out, while the latter saw only limited service. However this was enough to put in some spectacular performances – such as a non-stop Berlin-New York flight in August 1938 in just over 24 hours, while the return flight, with the prevailing winds, was made in 19hr 47min. Another Fw200 made a flight from Berlin to Tokyo with only two refuelling stops in a flight time of 42hr 18min. The potentialities were not lost on the Luftwaffe which modified the Condor as a long-range maritime patrol bomber; it would cause havoc to allied shipping during the early stage of the Battle of the Atlantic. A few Condors survived to see service as airliners after World War 2.

The Junkers Ju52/3m tri-motor was a direct descendent of the F13, W33 and W34. Originally designed as a single-engined cargo aircraft which appeared in 1930, the addition of two extra engines transformed the aircraft and the rest is history. Over 5,000 of the Tante Ju were built in Germany and, postwar, by Société Amiot in France and CASA in Spain. It served as transport, paratroop carrier, glider tug, bomber and military transport with the Luftwaffe in WW2, as well as an airliner with Lufthansa and various other airlines. With a maximum speed of 165mph, the Ju52/3m had a range of about 800 miles.

When looking at the development of air transport between the wars, one is inevitably drawn to North America where the greatest advances were made and where the foundations of the modern airliner were laid. Immediately after World War 1, America did not develop passenger carrying services to the extent that they were established in Europe, partly because of government restrictions. Instead much effort was put into the development of the aeroplane as a carrier of mail for the US Post Office. The huge distances, coupled with the extremes of climate encountered in the sub-continent, were important factors in the development of tough, practical and reliable aeroplanes. Initially, the aircraft were similar in concept to the contemporary European designs and, as already related, Fokker designs and their derivatives were best sellers in the States. However mailplanes gave many of today's manufacturers a start in the business of building commercial aircraft, a typical example being the Boeing Airplane Company, which built its first commercial aircraft, the Model 40 single-engined biplane, in 1925. In a successful bid to operate the San Francisco-Chicago portion of the transcontinental mail route in 1927, the Model 40 was extensively redesigned with a 420hp Pratt & Whitney radial engine. Thus equipped it could carry 1,200lb of mail and two passengers over a distance of 650 miles at a cruising speed of 92kts. Later versions carried four passengers and Boeing set up its own airline to fly this, and other, routes. Boeing Air Transport (BAT), as the company was named, grew rapidly and absorbed many other airlines before becoming United Airlines in 1931. In the meantime Boeing had built and flown its Model 80 tri-motor biplane in 1928. This could carry up to 12 passengers in its original form and 18 as the developed Model 80A. When the 80A entered service in 1929, BAT also introduced an important addition to airline customer service in the form of the world's first air hostesses.

The 1930s were years of great advances in aircraft design and the Boeing Model 200 Monomail set the trend for the new decade when it flew in May 1930. This clean single-engined all-metal monoplane had a retractable undercarriage and was 25kts faster than the Model 40, despite being powered by the same engine. Only a single Model 200 was built, but a better fate awaited the twin-engined Boeing Model 247 which flew in February 1933 and can be regarded as the world's first truly modern airliner. Powered by two 550hp Pratt & Whitney Wasp radials, the 247 had a crew of two and carried 10 passengers. It was of all-metal construction, had a retractable undercarriage and variable pitch propellers. Its performance was phenomenal for the time and with a cruising speed of 135kts it was considerably faster than aircraft such as the Fokker X and the Boeing Model 80 tri-motors. More significantly, its ability to maintain height and even climb at maximum weight on the power of one engine only offered a massive step forward in flight safety. Some 61 Boeing 247s were produced.

Boeing's last airliner built before the war was the massive four-engined Model 307 Stratoliner which was based on the contemporary B-17 Flying Fortress bomber. It featured a very roomy pressurised fuselage which could accommodate up to 33 seated passengers or 16 in convertible sleeper berths with a further nine in reclining seats. The introduction of a pressure cabin in a production civil airliner was another world first for Boeing and it could cruise at 195kts at altitudes up to 20,000ft, in the calmer air above the worst of the weather. The first orders came, in 1937, from Pan Am and TWA, and it began revenue earning flights in 1940. Apart from the destruction of the first Pan Am aircraft during testing, the other nine examples built ushered in a new era of safe and comfortable long range air services before being overtaken by the events of World War 2.

Another manufacturer which made its reputation in the years between the two world wars was the Lockheed Aircraft Company which, in 1927, flew an exceptionally clean single-engined high-wing monoplane named the Vega. The first example was intended as an entrant in the Dole Race from Oakland, California, to Hawaii and the standard four-seat passenger cabin was replaced with additional fuel tanks. The Vega 1 was powered by a 200hp

Wright Whirlwind radial engine and during preparations and trials for the Dole Race it established a number of records with payload and was the favourite to win when the eight contestants set off on 16 August 1927. Sadly, the Vega and its two pilots vanished over the vastness of the Pacific Ocean and the race was won by the Beech-designed Travel Air. However the potential of the Vega was widely recognised and subsequently 128 examples were built. The final Vega 5 was powered by a 450hp Wasp engine and could carry six passengers at speeds in excess of 140kts. Developments of the Vega included the Detroit Aircraft Corporation DL-1 with a metal instead of plywood fuselage, and the Lockheed Air Express which had a wing of increased span mounted parasol fashion above the fuselage. The Vega was sold to many US and foreign airlines and others were bought by private organisations. Several were used to establish some significant records, the most famous being a Vega 5B named *Winnie Mae* which took-off from New York on 23 June 1931 and flew around the world in only 8 days 15hr 51min, while the famous record breaking aviatrix Amilia Earhart used several Vegas during her career.

The success of the Vega established Lockheed as a major manufacturer and the company subsequently concentrated on a range of high-speed monoplanes mainly intended for mail flights or military use. However much of the technology used in these projects was incorporated into the Lockheed Orion, a single-engined low-wing monoplane with a retractable undercarriage which first flew in the spring of 1931. Seating six passengers in a comfortable cabin, the Orion was powered by a 450hp Wasp radial engine and could cruise at over 150kts. Although only 35 Orions were built, they saw extensive service with several US airlines and set a pattern which was copied by several other contemporary designs such as the Clark GA43 and the Northrop Delta 1-D. However the days of the single-engined airliner were numbered and in 1934 the US aviation authorities decreed that single-engined aircraft could not be used for the transport of passengers at night or over hazardous terrain. Even before this date, Lockheed was facing intense competition from other designs such as the Boeing 247. It developed, therefore, an elegant 10-passenger twin-engined aircraft called the Model 10 Electra. This took to the air in 1943 and was an immediate success, not least because of its 165kt cruising speed. Powered by two 450hp Pratt & Whitney Wasp radials, the Electra was an all-metal design and had advanced features such as variable pitch propellers, a retractable undercarriage and trailing edge split flaps. Some 148 Electras were produced and customers included Northwest Airlines and Pan Am, while many European air-

The Woolaroc Travel Air Model 5000 was a five-seat monoplane. Powered by a Wright Whirlwind J-5, 200hp engine, it was the winner of the 1927 Dole Race from the US mainland to Hawaii – beating the pre-race favourite, the Lockheed Vega.

lines – including KLM and British Airways – beat a path to Lockheed's door. It was in a British Airways' Electra that Prime Minister Neville Chamberlain made his flight to Munich to negotiate with Hitler, returning with an infamous piece of paper and announcing 'Peace in our time!'

The Electra was followed by the smaller Model 12 Electra Junior which, although smaller and lighter, retained the two Wasp radials and consequently showed a significant increase in performance, a fact not unnoticed by the world's military authorities. Some Model 12s, supposedly ordered by British Airways, were in fact used on behalf of the British and French intelligence agencies by pilot Sidney Cotton to carry out clandestine photographic reconnaissance missions over Germany and Italy prior to the outbreak of war. Lockheed's final pre-war airliner was the Model 14 Super Electra which could carry 14 passengers in a deepened fuselage, while more powerful 875hp Pratt & Whitney Hornet radial engines gave a cruising speed of 187kts over a range of 1,500 miles. The Model 14 flew in 1937 and 112 were built, customers including Continental, Northwest, Aer Lingus, KLM, Trans Canada and British Airways/BOAC. Further development of the basic design led to the larger 18-seater Model 18 Lodestar in 1940 which, although gaining many airline orders, was mainly built as a military transport for the US forces during the war.

Apart from the Boeing and Lockheed products, there were numerous other US airliners of the interwar period. Among the best known was the Ford 4-AT all-metal tri-motor which flew in 1926, powered by three 2,090hp Wright J4 Whirlwind radial engines: it carried a crew of two and eight passengers. Its all-metal construction, with distinctive corrugated skin panels (similar to that pioneered by the German Junkers company) earned it the fond nickname of 'Tin Goose'. Ford produced a total of 198 tri-motors between 1926 and 1931 and the basic design was continually improved so that the last model, the 5-AT, could carry up to 17 passengers and was powered by three 420hp Pratt & Whitney Wasp radials. However, with a cruising speed of only around 105kts and range with payload less than 500 miles, the tri-motor was rapidly eclipsed by the new twin-engined designs produced in the 1930s. Despite this the old Tin Goose is remembered with fondness and nostalgia, and one or two examples are still used for pleasure flying, serving as a reminder of how much air transport has changed in a few decades. Another well known airliner of the interwar period was the Curtiss Condor which flew in 1929 and, as the redesigned Condor II, in 1933. Carrying around 18 passengers, the twin-engined Condor was something of an intermediate stage in

The DC-2 first flew in 1934 and about 200 were built by Douglas in the USA and Nakajima in Japan. It could carry 14 passengers at a top speed of nearly 200mph to a range of 1,000 miles. It had a special de-icing system with Goodyear rubber de-icing boots along the wing and tail surfaces which were pulsated by air pressure to break up the ice when it formed. These weren't entirely successful and icing would remain a problem until the advent of gas turbines. Here a KLM DC-2 at Croydon airport.

airliner development as it retained the traditional biplane layout but married this to modern reliable powerplants (later with variable pitch propellers) and a retractable undercarriage. Its comfortable and roomy fuselage was popular with passengers but its performance was thoroughly eclipsed by the new all-metal monoplanes of the 1930s and the last of 45 Condors was delivered in 1934. Interestingly, some were subsequently bought by a British company, International Air Freight, which used them on freight services around Europe in 1937-38 when they were purchased by the Air Ministry, although they never flew again and were subsequently scrapped.

While Boeing and Lockheed were laying the foundations of their later successes, it was left to another company to produce what is widely regarded as the most significant milestone in the history of air transport and an aircraft which was produced in far greater numbers than any other airliner. The aircraft in question was the legendary DC-3 and its builder was the Douglas Aircraft Company based at Santa Monica, California. In the early 1930s Boeing had set the pace with its Model 247 which, initially, was destined for service with Boeing's sister company, United Airlines. Other airlines, notably TWA, realised that United would have a significant commercial advantage and immediately looked around for a suitable rival design. In 1932 TWA set out a demanding specification for an aircraft which would carry 12 passengers in comfortable accommodation over a distance of 1,000 miles at a speed of 125kts. Despite TWA's preference on safety grounds for a traditional tri-motor layout, Douglas was able to meet these requirements with its twin-engined Douglas Commercial 1, abbreviated to DC-1. It flew on 1 July 1933 powered originally by two 700hp Pratt & Whitney Hornet radial engines but these were later replaced by 710hp Wright Cyclones; in this form it showed a 30kt improvement over the cruising speed of the Boeing 247 and had a much greater range. The single DC-1 was delivered to TWA in September 1933 and the following year it was used to establish some highly publicised transcontinental speed records. In the meantime it was realised that the basic design could be developed without any significant performance loss and the result was the slightly longer DC-2 which could seat 14 passengers and had slightly more powerful Cyclone engines. This entered service with TWA in May 1934 and was subsequently sold to American Airlines, Eastern Air Lines, General Airlines, Pan American and Panagra. Overseas customers included KLM, Australian National Airlines, Canto Airlines (China), LAPE and Iberia (Spain), Swissair and many others. In Europe, production licences were obtained by Airspeed in the UK and Fokker in the Netherlands and although neither actually built any such aircraft, Fokker did act as a very successful sales agent for Douglas.

Although a reasonable commercial success (some 200 were built) the DC-2 achieved its greatest moment of fame in the unlikely setting of the MacRobertson Air Race from England to Australia in 1934. Starting from the new RAF station at Mildenhall, the race drew a wide range of entrants and the outright favourite was the specially built twin-engined two-seater de Havilland Comet. This was purely designed as a long distance racer and had no commercial pretensions. However the big surprise, at least to European observers unfamiliar with the pace of development in the United States, was the outstanding performance of the KLM-entered DC-2 which carried three passengers and 30,000 air mail letters during the race, winning the transport class by a handsome margin and finishing only a few hours behind the Comet which was the outright winner. This success alone would have guaranteed the Douglas company a string of orders for years ahead had it not been for the fact that an even more capable aircraft was about to take to the skies.

By 1934 American Airlines had introduced the concept of providing sleeping accommodation for its long range transcontinental flights. It was using its latest Condor 32 biplanes, whose capacious fuselage made them ideal for this role although their performance, at least in terms of cruising speed, was considerably less than that of the new monoplanes. American therefore asked Douglas to produce a sleeper version of the DC-2 which would have a wider

Possibly the most important commercial aircraft ever built, the DC-3 established air transport as a normal means of travel for thousands of travellers both during wartime and afterwards, as the many war surplus military aircraft were used by civil operators to transport men and cargo around the postwar world. In 1939 90 percent of the world's airline passengers flew in DC-3s. During the war – known as Skytrain, Skytrooper or Dakota – it served as transport, paratroop dropper, ambulance and glider tug. Postwar the DC-3 was used by both military and civil operators – there were 1,740 in commercial service in 1948 and it is still in use by more than 100 airlines today.

and longer fuselage to accommodate 14 sleeper berths. This was done and a number of other aerodynamic refinements were introduced in the Douglas Sleeper Transport (DST) which flew on 17 December 1935; a normally configured 21-seater version was known as the DC-3. A choice of powerplants was offered, either Wright Cyclones or Pratt & Whitney Twin Wasps, both giving approximately 1,000hp, and the type quickly became the world's best selling airliner with airlines clamouring to place orders. The reason for this was that, in building the DC-3, Douglas had created the first airliner which was capable of giving its owners and operators a profit without the need for any form of subsidy or Government sponsorship. Within two years of its first flight, the DC-3 was carrying 95 percent of all US airline passenger traffic and, in addition, was in service with over 30 foreign airlines. By the time that America entered World War 2 in 1941, over 450 DC-3s had been built (including 38 DSTs). Most of these were for civil use but from September 1940 the production lines were swollen with immense orders for military versions. Eventually over 13,000 civil DC-3s and military C-47s were built before US production finally ceased in 1947. This total included 485 built under licence in Japan and an estimated 2,000 produced in the Soviet Union as the Lisunov Li-2. The importance of the DC-3 to commercial air transport cannot be overstated. Already a major success before World War 2, the enormous number of surplus military aircraft after the war kept airlines supplied with a workhorse well into the 1960s, and even then many aircraft continued in use with third level airlines carrying passengers and cargo all over the world while the aircraft industry desperately strived to attain the 'holy grail' and produce a DC-3 replacement – nobody ever did.

Douglas did not rest on its laurels and, in conjunction with several US airlines, designed and flew the four-engined DC-4E in 1939. This was an extremely advanced design and was one of the first airliners to utilise a tricycle undercarriage. However, this original DC-4 was large, heavy and technically complex and would not have been suitable for airline service in its original form although it showed the way to the future and laid the foundation for Douglas's subsequent postwar success.

While this account has traced the history of the fixed wing landplane as an airliner from the end of World War 1 to the outbreak of World War 2 at the end of the 1930s, it should not be forgotten that other forms of air transport had their brief heyday. Of these the most ephemeral, perhaps, was the airship, which had seen considerable development as a military weapon and maritime patrol platform during World War 1. Its great assets, compared to the aeroplanes of the time, were its much greater load carrying ability and its endurance which held out the prospect of comfortable long range air travel. During the 1920s, the

Germans held the lead in airship development based on their experience with the wartime Zeppelins and other countries attempted to follow them. In Britain two major designs were commissioned. The government-sponsored R101 was completed in 1929 at a cost of £700,000 but was subject to much criticism in respect of its design and build quality, and it was seriously underpowered. Despite this it was dispatched on a flight to India on 4 October 1930 carrying the new Viceroy and several government officials including Lord Thompson, the Secretary of State for Air. In the early hours of the following morning it crashed near Beauvais in northern France and all 48 passengers and crew were killed. This effectively ended British commercial airship development despite the fact that the rival R100 built by Vickers proved to be much more durable because of its geodetic construction and more powerful engines. For many years German airships reigned supreme, particularly on the prestige route from Berlin to New York, the only commercially available aerial crossing available at that time. However the horrific and well publicised loss of the *Hindenburg* at Lakehurst, New Jersey, on 6 May 1937 finally ended the commercial career of the airship. Thirty-six people were killed when the stately airship burst into flames as it approached its mooring mast after a routine transatlantic crossing; newsreel film of the tragedy was shown around the world.

While the airship proved to be no competitor to the landplane, there was another rival which had a brief period of glory in the late 1930s: the long range flying boat. For a while it seemed to hold the key to long range air transport and was the subject of considerable development on both sides of the Atlantic. With the technology available prior to World War 2, it seemed impossible that a conventional aeroplane could carry a worthwhile payload together with the tons of fuel required for long range flights (such as across the Atlantic) and be able to take-off from the relatively small airfields of the day. This was primarily a function of the limited power available from contemporary engines, most of which produced less than 1,000hp. The flying boat seemed to offer a solution as it could operate from any suitable stretch of water with no physical restriction on the length of take-off run available. Nor did it require expensive runways or prepared surfaces to bear the weight of these large machines. As far as Britain was concerned, the flying boat also appeared well suited to providing air services to far-flung parts of the Empire where sophisticated land aerodromes were not available. One of the first British large commercial flying boats was the Short Calcutta which was built to meet an Imperial Airways requirement and first flew in February 1928. Based on the military Singapore, the Calcutta was a three-engined biplane with a maximum all-up weight of 22,500lb: it could carry 15 passengers in great luxury. Other accommodation features included a bar, galley, washroom and toilet while the crew consisted of two pilots, one of whom acted as radio operator and navigator, and a steward. Imperial Airways eventually operated five Calcuttas which were mainly used on services across the Mediterranean, from Genoa to Alexandria. Political problems later led to the withdrawal of facilities in Italy and Imperial Airways subsequently ordered three new flying boats which were basically enlarged Calcuttas powered by four engines, the new type being known as the Kent and all three were delivered in 1931.

However the greatest step forward followed a Government decision to carry all mail throughout the Empire without surcharge. This required a fleet of powerful aircraft capable of carrying heavy loads and the result was the classic Short S23 'Empire' class flying boat. The prototype, named *Canopus*, flew on 4 July 1936 by which time Imperial Airways had already ordered 28 and by 1938 the Empire boats were operating seven services a week to Egypt, four a week to India and another three to East Africa. South Africa, Malaya, Hong Kong and Australia were each served twice weekly. In the course of operating these services, the new flying boats replaced the antique fleet of landplanes which had made up much of the Imperial Airways' fleet and the Empire C class was very much the wonder of the age, viewed by the public in much the same manner as Concorde is today. Powered by four 920hp Bristol Pegasus radial engines, the Empire boats cruised at a respectable 145kts and

The fine lines of the Empire class flying boats are shown off in this Short Bros photograph of Ao Tea Roa, which first flew on 18 April 1939. It was one of the nine S30s which were built with heavier engines – 890hp Bristol Perseus XIICs. Ao Tea Roa retired from service on 29 October 1947 having flown 1,230,000 miles with Tasman. It became a coffee bar at Mechanics Bay, Auckland, a slightly ignominious end for such a beautiful airliner. The Empire class flying boats could carry up to 24 passengers, had a cruising speed of 165mph and a range of 1,300 miles.

had a range of 750 miles. They could carry up to 24 passengers, although this was normally reduced to around 16 to allow the installation of sleeping bunks and the carriage of cargo and mail. The Australian airline Qantas took delivery of three C class, bringing the total production of this version to 31 aircraft. Also built were four Bristol Perseus-powered S30s, which had a range of 1,300 miles, and two S33s, the latter strengthened to allow a maximum take-off weight of 53,000lb. Despite this success, the standard C class was not capable of flying passengers across the Atlantic although two aircraft were modified with long range tanks and were used to conduct a series of trial flights without any payload across the Atlantic in 1937. Later some of the S30s were modified to allow air-to-air refuelling from converted Handley Page Harrow bombers and in this guise flew some transatlantic commercial mail flights before the outbreak of war in 1939.

The final prewar development of the Short flying boat was the S26 G class of which only three were built. Powered by four 1,380hp Bristol Hercules engines, these magnificent aircraft had a take-off weight of 73,500lb and a range of 3,200 miles at a cruising speed of 157kts. Although capable of carrying up to 40 passengers, Imperial Airways intended to use them on non-stop transatlantic mail flights but by the time the first aircraft, named *Golden Hind*, flew in July 1939 the clouds of war were gathering and all three were requisitioned for service with the RAF. Of the three, only *Golden Hind* survived the war and was briefly used as a 38-seater civil airliner until retired at the end of 1947.

In Europe both France and Germany developed various flying boats of which the most unusual was the giant 12-engined Dornier X which flew in 1929 and made a tremendous impression when it visited the United Sates in 1931. However more successful were the twin-engined Dornier Wal and Dornier 18 which were used extensively on long range mail flights to South America, often being flown off specially constructed catapult ships.

Many successful flying boats were also developed in the United States, mainly for use across the vastness of the Pacific Ocean. Some of the best designs were the four-engined Martin M-130 which entered service in 1935 flying mail with Pan Am, and the Sikorsky S42 which flew in 1934 powered by four 700hp Pratt & Whitney Hornets and cruised at 120kts. Neither of these boats was quite in the same class as the British 'Empire' boats, but Pan Am had set out a specification for a transoceanic flying boat in 1935 and the result was the 82,500lb Boeing Model 314 Clipper. It flew first in June 1938 and began the first passenger carrying transatlantic air service on 28 June 1939. The deep hull could accommodate up to 74 passengers although 40 was the normal load on long distance flights and a total of 12 was built before construction ceased in 1941. Three of these aircraft were purchased from Pan Am by BOAC and flew transatlantic services throughout the war. The Model 314 was powered by four 1,200hp (1,500hp for take-off) Wright GR-2600 Double Cyclone radial engines which gave it a range of 3,500 miles at a cruising speed of 160kts. An unusual feature of the aircraft was the use of fuselage sponsons, instead of wingtip floats, to provide stability on the water, and it also had the distinction of being the largest production aircraft in regular airline service in the world at the time, an achievement which Boeing was to repeat in the future.

By the end of the 1930s all the elements of a modern air transport system were in place: aircraft were of all-metal construction and were carrying heavier loads higher, faster and over greater distances. Safety had reached a level which encouraged people to fly and a network of airports had sprung up around the world. The first electronic navigation aids were being installed while the first true long haul air services had just begun. Sadly, the enormous progress made in only 20 years was roughly brushed aside as the world fell into the abyss of World War 2 and, for all practical purpose, the development of commercial aviation came to a temporary halt. When peace dawned in 1945, the world was a different place and there were substantial changes in the nature of the aircraft which would be required.

1945 to 1960 (US)

The upheaval of World War 2 brought substantial and far reaching changes to the air transport industry. On the one hand the technological advances of the war years set the scene for new aircraft which completely outclassed their predecessors in terms of both size and performance, while on the other the sheer global extent of the war had broadened people's minds to the concept of travel. The result was a steadily increasing demand for air travel which was sustained by the emergence of new aircraft offering greater speed, comfort and safety. The most prestigious route rapidly became the transatlantic crossing between the United States and war-torn Europe, a route which had been pioneered on a small scale by flying boats in the late 1930s but which could now be flown regularly by the new breed of four-engined landplanes. These benefited from the priceless experience of the military Atlantic Air Ferry operation during the war, when crossing the Atlantic changed from a risky adventure to, literally, an everyday operation. A legacy of this was the infrastructure of airfields and navigation procedures which was now available for civil use, including such famous places as Prestwick, Shannon and Gander and aids such as Con sol, Loran and ILS.

The story of the Armstrong Whitworth AW27 Ensign class shows how easy it is to waste a lot of time and money in the aviation world. Designed to meet the needs of the 1934 Empire Air Mail scheme, continued changes demanded by the airline – Imperial – a host of technical problems and the priority that had to be given to Armstrong Whitworth's bomber, the Whitley, as Britain rearmed for war all conspired to delay the first prototype flight till 24 January 1938. It was soon realised that the aircraft was underpowered and that it had a slow rate of climb because of the length of time it took to retract the undercarriage. The subsequent modifications delayed route-proving trials until October and that Christmas three of the class were chosen for mail flights to Australia. The results were not impressive: Egeria needed an engine change at Athens, Elsinore one at Karachi and Euterpe only just reached India. Immediately after the war the seven survivors of the 14-strong class were broken up. Here Euryalus taxies across the road from the AW air service training workshops to Hamble airfield prior to its first flight on 18 August 1939.

So successful were the twin-engined, metal monoplanes like the DC-2 and Boeing 247 that thoughts began to turn to four-engined versions. Douglas started discussions with five US airlines – United, American, TWA, Eastern and Pan Am – all of which put up $100,000 each towards the cost of development. The resulting Douglas DC-4 was so completely different to the final version that it was later given the suffix E for experimental. It was larger, its wing was nearly 21ft longer, it had three tail fins and rudders and it first flew on 7 June 1938. Painted in United's livery, the DC-4E began proving flights but was a disappointment. The decision was made to produce a single tail-finned, reduced size version and the DC-4E ended up in Japan. The redesigned DC-4 was also notable for having the first transport fuselage with a long parallel section of constant diameter: this would enable the aircraft to be stretched into DC-6 and DC-7 versions. The programme was taken over by the military after Pearl Harbor and the DC-4 became the C-54 Skymaster. There were nine military and naval versions and many of these came onto the market post-WW2, a factor in keeping the Douglas commercial production figure to a paltry 79: 1,236 were built for the military.

The country ideally placed to take advantage of this new opportunity was the United States whose aircraft industry had produced vast numbers of transport aircraft and bombers during the war; many of them were suitable for development as civil airliners. It was in this era that famous aircraft such as the Boeing Stratocruiser and the Lockheed Constellation entered service, but there was one manufacturer which reigned supreme for over a decade and whose name became almost synonymous with commercial transports. It was, of course, the Santa Monica-based Douglas Aircraft Company which had made its name before the war with the famous DC-3 that, in its military guises as the C-47, Skytrain or Dakota, became the standard transport aircraft of the allied powers. After the war, surplus military DC-3/C-47s went on to become the backbone of the civil air fleet throughout the world with some examples still flying today. However the DC-3 was essentially a short range aircraft and was incapable of flying any worthwhile payload safely across the Atlantic; it was its four-engined successor, the DC-4, which catapulted Douglas into the forefront of the transatlantic market.

As already described, the original DC-4 – later given the suffix E for Experimaental – first flew in 1938 but proved to be too complex for its time: simply, its performance was unexciting. After consultation with various airlines including Eastern, American and United, Douglas decided to abandon the DC-4E and develop a lighter version which would be cheaper, easier to maintain and offer better performance characteristics. The result was to become a classic shape in the skies. Featuring a circular section fuselage with a single square-shaped fin, the new DC-4 had an efficient high aspect tapered wing and was to be powered by four radial piston engines, either the 1,000hp Wright Cyclone or the 1,050hp Pratt & Whitney Twin Wasp. In fact production versions were powered by the developed Pratt & Whitney R2000 Twin Wasp which produced 1,450hp and gave the aircraft a typical cruising speed of 177kts and the ability to carry a maximum payload of 14,200lb. These figures were naturally of great interest to the US Army Air Force (and the British purchasing commission) and by the time that the first prototype flew on 14 February 1942, all thoughts of producing a civil airliner had been put aside; the aircraft was built as the C-54 Skymaster. Production mounted rapidly with 24 being delivered in 1942, 74 in 1943, 354 in 1944 and no fewer than 710 in 1945. At the end of the war, Douglas was therefore in a commanding position to supply the airlines with new aircraft, especially as it had a massive stockpile of components prepared for further cancelled military orders. In the event, only 79 new build civil DC-4s were completed and production ceased in 1947, the main reason being the large

number of surplus military aircraft which became available. However the new aircraft went to several major airlines including Western, National and Northwest in the United States and Sabena, Air France, Iberia, KLM and Swissair in Europe. The last DC-4 from the Santa Monica production line went to South African Airlines on 9 August 1947. In addition, surplus C-54s were bought by numerous airlines and one of these, American Overseas Airlines, initiated the first commercial transatlantic landplane service on 23 October 1945. It flew between New York and Britain's Hurn airport in 23hr 18min flying time with technical stops to refuel at Gander and Shannon – a pattern of transatlantic flying which persisted into the jet age. It is interesting to note that six other airlines (Pan Am, Air France, Sabena, KLM, SAS and Swissair) also initiated their postwar transatlantic services with the DC-4, while in the United States airlines such as Braniff, Capital, Delta and TWA (to name but a few) began using the aircraft on domestic and transcontinental services. The standard accommodation on the DC-4 was for four flight crew and 44 passengers and cabin attendants. However airlines varied in their seating arrangements and some aircraft used on high density domestic routes carried as many as 86 passengers.

The Douglas DC-4 spawned a couple of interesting developments, the most important of which was built under licence at Montreal by Canadair Ltd. It was powered by four 1,760hp Rolls-Royce Merlin 622 engines, which resulted in the designation DC-4M for this variant. Not only was the Merlin-powered version faster in the cruise by some 50kts, it was also pressurised and therefore offered greater comfort to its passengers. Consequently this version was ordered by BOAC to replace its disaster-prone Avro Tudors, the use of a substantial amount of British equipment including the engines resulting in a considerable and important reduction in the dollar cast of each aircraft. BOAC received the first of 22 aircraft, known as the Argonaut in service, in March 1949 and the last example was not retired until as late as 1960. Accommodation was provided for 40 first class passengers or up to 62 in economy seating. Other airline customers for the DC-4M included Trans-Canada Airlines and Canadian Pacific Airlines.

The other DC-4 derivative was the unique AT(E)L-98 Carvair, a conversion carried out by Aviation Traders Engineering at Southend in England. These aircraft were designed as car ferries to replace the Bristol Superfreighters of Channel Air Bridge and Silver City Airlines and featured a new bulbous nose which moved the flightdeck above the line of the fuselage so that a straight through cargo compartment could be loaded through a side-hinging front cargo door. A total of 21 such conversions was completed between 1962 and 1968 and they saw service with various airlines in 10 countries, although none are flying today.

Despite the pioneering services flown by various DC-4s, the type was already being superseded in the late 1940s by its big brother, the Douglas DC-6. This was a fairly straightforward development of the DC-4: design work began in 1944 with the maiden flight occurring at Santa Monica on 15 February 1946. The DC-6 followed the general outline of the earlier aircraft and used the same wing, strengthened to cope with a longer, pressurised, fuselage and a maximum take-off weight of 97,000lb, up from the 73,000lb of the DC-4. More powerful (2,100hp) Pratt & Whitney R-2800-34 Double Wasp radial engines provided a substantial boost in performance, cruising speed rising to 285kts and range with maximum payload being over 3,000 miles. The original DC-6 model was only 7ft longer than the DC-4 and normal seating was for 48-52 passengers, although more could be carried in a high-density layout. However the DC-6 did not have an auspicious start to its career and two serious inflight fires shortly after it entered service with United Airlines in April 1947 resulted in the aircraft being grounded for four months. Once the cause had been established and rectified the aircraft went on to become extremely reliable and the DC-6 family earned a reputation as the most economic of the postwar piston-engined airliners.

The basic design was developed as the DC-6A, a pressurised all cargo variant which had the fuselage stretched to a length of 105ft 7in and was powered by new 2,400hp Pratt &

Whitney Double Wasps. Maximum payload was 28,188lb which could be carried almost 3,000 miles. Although some of these aircraft were subsequently converted to passenger use, the true airliner variant was the DC-6B which was identical except that it did not feature the strengthened cargo floor and the upward opening freight doors, and had accommodation for between 54 and 102 passengers depending on the configuration. A total of 704 DC-6s of all variants (including the military C-118 and R6D-1) was built including no less than 288 DC-6Bs, which were bought by many of the world's major airlines including Pan Am, Braniff, Swissair, Canadian Pacific, Japan Airlines, SAS and Alitalia. The last was delivered to JAT (Jugoslovenski Aerotransport) in November 1958. A convertible freight/passenger version was designated the DC-6C.

While airlines flocked to buy the DC-4 and DC-6, Douglas realised that the new 3,250hp Wright R-3350 turbo compound engines, which were to power the new Lockheed Super Constellation, would offer significant improvements in range, speed and payload. At the instigation of American Airlines, the company set about adapting the basic DC-6 design to take the more powerful engines, the result being the DC-7 which took to the air in May 1953 and had a fuselage lengthened to 108ft 11in. Gross take-off weight was 122,200lb and passenger capacity was between 69 and 95. A total of 105 DC-7s was built, all of which went to major US airlines – United, American, Delta and National – for use on domestic routes. The DC-7B, which flew in October 1954, had a higher gross weight (126,000lb) and carried more fuel, enabling it to fly on the all important transatlantic route. Pan Am started non-stop New York-London services on 13 June 1955 and other customers included South African Airways, American Airlines, Eastern and Continental. 112 of this version were built and these were followed by 121 of the ultimate development of the Douglas piston-engined airliner – the DC-7C, known from its designation as the Seven Seas. This first flew on 20 December 1955 and, with a maximum weight of 143,000lb, was powered by four 3,400hp Wright R-3350-18EA-1 turbo compound radials giving it a cruising speed of just over 300kts and a range with maximum payload (23,350lb) of 4,605 miles. This performance made it the first truly intercontinental airliner capable of crossing the Atlantic non-stop in either direction against the prevailing headwinds. It also pioneered commercial great circle routes over the Polar regions and was the first airliner capable of non-stop flights across America from New York to the West Coast. The success of Pan Am on the transatlantic routes meant that rival airlines such as BOAC, Sabena, Alitalia, SAS, KLM and Swissair were also forced to buy the aircraft in order to remain competitive. The last DC-7C was delivered to KLM on 10 December 1958 by which time the air transport world was on the threshold of the true jet age, and the aircraft's career as a prestige airliner was relatively short.

While Douglas remained the foremost producer of four-engined airliners, building a total of 2,355 DC-4/6/7s including military production, it was not without competition. One rival was the mighty Boeing company which, although occupied with massive military contracts for aircraft such as the B-50 developed from the wartime B-29 and the new jet-powered B-47 Stratojet, was also building the KC-97 tanker/transport for the United States Air Force. The KC-97 was also developed from the B-29 bomber and used the same 3,500hp Pratt & Whitney R-4360 Double Wasp four-row radial powerplants as the later B-50. The bomber's wings and tail assembly were mated to a new curvaceous double-bubble cross-sectioned pressurised fuselage. Almost 900 were built between 1944, when the prototype flew, and 1956 when production ceased in favour of the new jet KC-135. The first commercial version, the Boeing Model 377 Stratocruiser, flew on 8 July 1947 but it did not emulate the success of its military counterpart and only 55 aircraft were built, including 20 for Pan Am and six for BOAC, although the British airline eventually operated 17 Stratocruisers having bought others from SAS and United Airlines. Production ended in March 1950. Despite being built in small numbers, the Stratocruiser became well known amongst travellers of the period due to its distinctive shape and the novel feature of a fully fledged and spacious cocktail bar on

the lower deck. It could carry between 60 and 112 passengers depending on the layout and it had a great impact on people's concept of air travel, introducing standards of comfort which would not be equalled for another two decades.

A more significant competitor for Douglas was Lockheed, which produced the graceful four-engined triple-tailed Constellation, surely one of the most beautiful aircraft ever to fly. Like the DC-4, the Constellation had its origins back in the immediate prewar period and was designed to the requirements of TWA and Pan Am but by the time it first flew in January 1943 it was as a military transport, the C-69. However only a few had been delivered by the end of the war and many on order were made available to civil operators as the Lockheed L049, the first going to Pan Am and TWA, while five went to BOAC, both of the latter airlines commencing transatlantic services in the course of 1946. Like the DC-6, the Constellation had its teething problems and was grounded for a short period in the summer of 1946 following a series of on-board fires. The first true civil version was the Model 649 which flew on 19 October 1946. It was powered by four 2,500hp Wright R-3350-C18B Duplex Cyclones giving it a cruising speed of 255kts but only 14 were delivered before production switched to the L749 which had additional fuel tankage in the wings and a strengthened undercarriage to permit operations at a gross weight of 107,000lb. This version could carry between 48 and 64 passengers over distances up to 3,500 miles, over 1,000 miles more than the L649, while a high density version had seating for 81. Some 74 L749 Constellations were built and it was flown by many major airlines including Air France, KLM, Eastern Airlines and BOAC.

With the advent of aircraft such as the Stratocruiser, Constellation, and DC-4/6, the market for air travel began to grow rapidly and the airlines began to write specifications for larger and longer ranged aircraft. To meet such requirements Lockheed developed the Model L1049 Super Constellation which, as well as having a fuselage stretched by over 18ft to increase maximum seating capacity to 109, also had a strengthened airframe, increased fuel capacity, large cabin windows and more powerful 2,700hp R-3350-956C-18CB engines. In this guise it entered service with Eastern Airlines in 1951 but proved to be underpowered. The subsequent L1049C was fitted with 3,250hp R-3350-972TC-18DA Turbo Cyclone engines, KLM being the lead customer, inaugurating an Amsterdam-New York service in August 1953. The new Super Constellation proved extremely popular, its eyecatching appeal giving the airlines which flew it an immediate marketing advantage, and several further variants were

The Douglas DC-6 was a stretched – just over 2m (7ft) longer – DC-4 with more powerful engines and pressurisation, which allowed for a more economical cruising altitude and which also had the added benefit of improving the passengers' ride because the aircraft could fly over the weather. The design started at the end of WW2 under the USAAF designation XC-112 but it saw only civil service, flying for the first time on 15 February 1946. Production ran to 537, of which the bulk (288) was the DC-6B. The most economical piston-engined airliner of the 1950s, it was introduced to transcontinental services in April 1951.

The battle between Lockheed and Douglas for the postwar commercial aviation market led to the Lockheed L1049 Super Constellation, along with the L749 Constellation one of the most beautiful piston-engined aircraft ever produced. The most successful civil version of the Super Constellation was the L1049G, 103 of which were built at Burbank. Super Constellation production finished up at 579 aircraft, of which 320 were military variants. The L1049G had 3,400hp Wright 972TC-18DA-3 Turbo Compound engines giving a max speed of 370mph and a 305mph cruising speed; for long-range operations the total tankage (with the 600 US gal wingtip tanks) was 7,750gal allowing a max range of 4,810 miles. Max take-off weight increased to 137,500lb – making their 'Super G' nickname accurate in size as well as performance. The L1049H was a freighter version of the G.

produced including the L1049G (sometimes referred to as the Super G) which could be distinguished by large external wing tanks – the only example of these being fitted to a major commercial airliner.

The ultimate development of the Constellation, and a contemporary of the rival DC-7C, was the L1649 Starliner. Although based on the Super Constellation, it featured an entirely new high aspect wing of increased span and fuel capacity, doing away with the need for tip tanks and bestowing a range of 6,320 miles at a cruising speed of 300kts. The new wing also allowed the aircraft to cruise at higher altitudes and the increased span permitted the engines to be moved outboard, reducing cabin noise The result was the smoothest of the piston-engined airliners and one which soldiered on into the jet era before being replaced. The 43 Starliners built were delivered to TWA, Lufthansa and Air France. A total of 935 Constellations of all variants (including military) was built, of which no less than 595 were L1049 Super Constellations. Production ceased in 1958.

Although the big four-engined airliners were the glamorous icons of this era, the American manufacturers had not neglected the need for smaller short and medium range aircraft to cover the multitude of commuter and business routes in the United States and international services in Europe and other parts of the world. However development of such aircraft was difficult in the face of the enormous numbers of ex-military DC-3s which provided a cheap and reliable workhorse to the world's smaller airlines and was extremely difficult to replace. One company which did succeed in producing a modern twin-engined medium sized airliner was Consolidated Vultee (later known as Convair) which had been responsible for the production of the B-24 Liberator bomber during World War 2. After the war it produced the 30-seater Convair 110 which first flew on 8 July 1946 and was powered by two 2,100hp Pratt & Whitney R-2800-S1C3-G radial engines. This did not find favour with the airlines and was developed into the 40-seater Convair 240 which had more powerful R-2800-CA18 engines and a considerably better performance, a combination which led to orders for 176 aircraft following its maiden flight in March 1947. Also known as the Convair Liner, the

CV240 had a high aspect wing for efficient cruise performance coupled with large high lift flaps for optimum field performance, and introduced a pressurised cabin and tricycle under-carriage to this class of airliner. A stretched and improved version, the CV340, first flew in October 1951 and with gross weight increased from 41,790lb to 47,000lb, it could carry 44 passengers over 2,015 miles at a speed of 245kts; 209 were produced to civil orders. The final production version was the CV440 Metropolitan which was stretched by a further 28in and could carry up to 52 passengers. It featured a number of refinements, including extensive soundproofing which improved both performance and passenger appeal. 155 were built. All three versions of the Convair Liner saw extensive service with numerous air-lines including United, Eastern, Continental, Sabena, Iberia and SAS, and the aircraft was also produced as a military transport and trainer.

The versatility of the Convair Liner, and a tribute to the soundness of the basic design, is illustrated by the fact that many of the aircraft were re-engined with turboprops and several continue in service up to the present. The first such conversion took place as early as 1954 and between then and 1962 those equipped with the British-built 3,060shp Napier Eland turboprop were designated CV540, while those fitted with US 3,750shp Allison 501 turbo-props became CV580s. Other popular conversions were the CV600 and CV640, powered by the ubiquitous Rolls-Royce Dart engine.

A potential rival to the Convair range was the Martin 2-0-2 and its successor, the 4-0-4. In fact the Martin 2-0-2 was the first to fly, on 13 August 1947, ahead of the Convair 240, and it entered service with LAN-Chile in October 1947. Although powered by the same Pratt & Whitney R-2800 engines and seating up to 40 passengers, the 2-0-2 was unpressurised and structural problems led to it being grounded for a period in 1948. Production of the 2-0-2 was halted and Martin concentrated on developing a slightly larger pressurised version known as the 4-0-4. This first flew in October 1951 and a total of 103 was built between 1951 and 1953, going mainly to TWA and Eastern Airlines. Its performance, which includ-ed a range of 1,080 miles at a cruising speed of 242kts with 40 passengers, compared unfavourably with the rival Convair design and no further orders were forthcoming.

1945-1960 (UK and Europe)

While the American manufacturers raced ahead and gained a virtual monopoly of the post-war airliner market, British companies struggled to adjust to peacetime conditions and tried to make up the lost ground. To meet an immediate need for aircraft to service the Empire and Commonwealth routes, several conversions of Lancaster and Halifax bombers were pressed into service. The crudest of these were six Lancasters delivered virtually unmodified except for the removal of the gun turrets to British South American Airways for use as freighters, although a more refined conversion was the Avro 691 Lancastrian which could carry up to 13 passengers in a civilianised fuselage with streamlined fairings replacing the nose and tail turrets and a row of cabin windows along each side. A more substantial derivative of the Lancaster was the Avro 685 York, which used the bomber's engines, wings and tailplane mated to a new low-slung square-section fuselage. The York was developed as a military transport and first flew in July 1942 but some were allocated to BOAC for use from 1944 onwards and others were flown by Skyways, British South American Airways and FAMA of Argentina. A total of 84 Yorks saw civil service and, surprisingly, BOAC did not retire its last example until as late as 1957, despite the availability of more modern aircraft.

Avro was well aware that converted bombers and military transports were not ideal for postwar airline operations and as early as 1943 had looked at a brand new design which eventually flew as the Tudor on 14 June 1945. This aircraft had the distinction of being Britain's first pressurised transport aircraft and, powered by four 1,770hp Rolls-Royce Merlin 621 piston engines, was intended to carry 12 passengers over 3,630 miles at a cruising speed of 183kts. Despite high hopes, the Tudor 1 proved to be a great disappointment and underwent a prolonged period of development before being rejected by BOAC in 1947, although a few were subsequently converted into Tudor 3s for use as government VIP transports. The rest were rebuilt as the stretched Tudor 4, seating 32 passengers, several of which were delivered to British South American Airways, which flew them briefly until two were lost in 1948 and 1949 in unexplained accidents near Bermuda (adding more fuel to the Bermuda Triangle legend). A larger version, designated the Tudor 2, had seating for up to 66 passengers in a fuselage stretched to 105ft 7in and in 1944 orders were placed for 79 aircraft by BOAC, Qantas and South African Airlines. However, when the prototype flew in March 1946 it displayed the same problems as its predecessors and the resulting modifications led to a substantial loss of performance which led to the cancellation of most of the original orders. The unhappy saga of the Tudor continued when the prototype Tudor 4 crashed on take-off at Woodford, killing four of the occupants including Roy Chadwick who had designed both the Tudor and the famous Lancaster. Despite further development work, the Tudor was finished as a commercial venture. The Lancaster's wartime partner had been the Handley Page Halifax bomber and this was also pressed into service as a transport aircraft in the postwar era. In fact a military cargo version, the Halifax C Mk 8, had already been developed and this became popular with air freight companies. A passenger version was produced for BOAC to cover shortages caused by the failure of the Tudor and 12 such conversions were carried out by Shorts at Belfast. Seating 10 passengers and carrying up to 8,000lb of freight, these aircraft were known as Haltons and flew on Middle East routes between 1946 and 1947.

However, like Avro, the Handley Page company was determined to produce a modern purpose-designed airliner and began work on the new HP68 Hermes 1 during the war. Powered by four Bristol Hercules radial engines and intended to carry 34-50 passengers in a pressurised fuselage, the prototype crashed on its maiden flight on 3 December 1945 and was completely destroyed. Despite this severe setback, development work continued and a military version known as the Hastings eventually served for many years with the RAF. The civil HP74 Hermes 2 prototype, which made a successful first flight on 2 September 1947, was 13ft longer than the Hermes 1 but still retained an obsolescent tailwheel configuration. However the production Hermes 4 featured a modern tricycle undercarriage and 25 were built for delivery to BOAC, entering revenue service in 1950 when they were deployed on the airline's routes in South and West Africa. Powered by four 2,100hp Bristol Hercules radials, they were configured to carry a crew of five and 40 passengers over 2,000 miles at a cruising speed of 240kts. After a short career they were mothballed in 1952 but some were reinstated following the withdrawal of the early Comets in 1954. Subsequently they served with a number of independent airlines until the early 1960s when they were scrapped.

The Hermes was designed during WW2 and when it entered service in 1950, it looked its age. BOAC was the only airline to take it, 25 of the Hermes 4 being bought for the route to South Africa. Its main strength was its ability to carry 63 passengers up to 3,500 miles, but both the Constellation and DC-6 were better aircraft. Apart from a new lease of life brought about by the Comet crashes, the Hermes saw little service with the major airlines but was used extensively as a trooper. Some Hermes 4s were upgraded to 4A standard with slightly more powerful engines. Most were scrapped in the early 1960s with 13 December 1964 the date of its final commercial flight.

The great symbol of British hopes to take the lead in airliner technology was the massive Bristol Brabazon, which had been conceived during World War 2 as a high speed airliner capable of carrying 100 passengers non-stop across the Atlantic in style and luxury. With a span of 230ft, a length of 177ft and a maximum take-off weight of 290,000lb, the Brabazon was indeed a magnificent project and the largest airliner ever built at that time, its overall dimensions only being equalled by Boeing's massive jet-powered 747 of the 1970s. The Brabazon Mk 1 flew on 4 September 1949 powered by no less than eight Bristol Centaurus radial piston engines coupled in pairs driving contra-rotating propellers. A Mk II was to have been powered by eight 3,500ehp Proteus turboprops but this version never flew and the prototype was broken up in 1953 after less than 400 hours' test flying. Whether the Brabazon could ever have been developed into a commercially viable aircraft is open to debate but the massive expense of the programme was the ultimate reason for its cancellation. The Brabazon had been named after Lord Brabazon who had chaired a committee set up in 1944 to determine the specifications for aircraft which would be needed by British airlines when the war ended and the massive project was the committee's Type 1. However some of the committee's other specifications resulted in more successful designs, one of which was the de Havilland DH104 Dove designed to meet Specification Type 5B as a replacement for the prewar Dragon Rapide. The Dove, which first flew in September 1945, was an immediate success and over 500 were built before production ended in 1968. Early airline customers for this attractive 8-11 seater included Hunting, Olley and Morton Air Services, while BOAC used a couple for crew training. The success of the Dove led to the development of a larger (14-17 seats) four-engined version, the DH114 Heron, which was produced as the Mk 1 with a fixed undercarriage and the Mk 2 with retractable wheels. 148 were built and many were modified and re-engined in the United States and Canada where the type was popular as a commuter airliner. The most extensive redesign was the Saunders ST-27, a Canadian derivative powered by two 750shp Pratt & Whitney (Canada) PT6A-34 turboprops which replaced the normal four 250hp de Havilland Gipsy Queen piston engines, while the fuselage was stretched to carry up to 23 passengers and a cabin attendant.

In the field of medium-sized airliners, British manufacturers had some moderate successes. The Vickers Viking was based on experience with the wartime Wellington twin-engined bomber, and the first Viking 1A, which flew in June 1945, employed the same wings and undercarriage mated to a tubby but spacious fuselage which could seat up to 21 passengers. Power was provided by two 1,690hp Bristol Hercules radials; the Viking 1B was similarly powered but had a 30in fuselage stretch to increase passenger capacity to 27 and a redesigned wing. Approximately 163 civil Vikings were built between 1945 and 1947, many going to BEA which used them throughout its early postwar European network while others were bought by airlines from Argentina, Africa, Denmark, Eire, India and Iraq as well as by other British airlines. The Viking was a sturdy and reliable aircraft but did little to advance airliner technology. A more pleasing design, but less successful in terms of sales, was the Airspeed Ambassador which resulted from the Brabazon Committee's specification IIA for a short haul airliner and which entered service with BEA in 1952, having flown in prototype form in 1947. It was powered by a pair of Centaurus 661 radial engines and could carry up to 50 passengers. The Ambassador, known as the Elizabethan in BEA service, featured a graceful pressurised fuselage with a distinctive triple tail, a shoulder-mounted high aspect wing and was one of the first British production airliners to have a modern tricycle undercarriage. It also proved economic to operate. Despite these attributes, no further orders were received after production of 20 aircraft for BEA, because of the impending introduction of the new turboprop airliners. Much more successful in terms of sales was the Bristol 170, also called the Freighter or Wayfarer, the latter being a 34-seater passenger version. This was a rugged no nonsense twin-engined aircraft designed mainly for the carriage of freight, which could be easily loaded via a pair of nose-mounted clamshell doors. The high wing lay-

The Bristol 170 Freighter prototype first flew in 1945; it was designed as a short-range military transport aircraft capable of landing small vehicles and supplies. Its twin nose doors opened on to a 49ft long x 8ft wide x 6ft 7in high cargo area which could take a standard British Army three-tonner. The second prototype was configured as a passenger carrier; dubbed the Wayfarer, in service it could carry up to 60 passengers (in its Super Wayfarer configuration). It is perhaps best known for its use as a car ferry between England and the Continent by Silver City Airways, whose first flight to France was on 13 July 1948 between Lympne and Le Touquet. Later the Freighter Mk 32 was developed for Silver City Airwys; it had space for three, rather than two, cars. A Bristol Freighter was also used to deliver vehicles of a different kind: light armoured vehicles into the beleaguered French fortress of Dien Bien Phu in 1953.

out allowed an unobstructed cargo bay and power was provided by two Bristol Hercules radial engines, initially rated at 1,690hp but giving up to 1,980hp in later versions, and the tailwheel undercarriage was fixed. The Type 170 first flew in December 1945 and the type remained in production until 1956 by which time 214 had been delivered, including 20 of the Mk 32 Superfreighters distinguishable by their elongated noses. These were used by Silver City Airways (and later British Air Ferries and Channel Air Bridge) on the pioneering car ferry services between southeast England and the European mainland. The Superfreighter could carry three cars together with drivers and passengers, while at least one was converted to 'Super Wayfarer' configuration and was fitted with seats for no fewer than 60 passengers! In its many versions the Bristol Freighter served airlines and air forces all over the world, but none now remain in revenue service and one of the last airworthy examples, restored to pristine condition, was unfortunately written off in a crash in the summer of 1996. Despite the failure of the Tudor, Hermes and Brabazon, Britain was about to take a substantial step forward in airliner technology through its lead in the application of gas turbine technology. In the late 1940s and early 1950s the British aircraft industry staked its future on the success of three airliner projects all of which utilised the jet engine and its turboprop derivative and which, it was hoped, would be far in advance of anything American industry could offer. These were the de Havilland Comet, the Vickers Viscount and the Bristol Britannia and their subsequent careers encompassed everything from outstanding commercial success to tragic failure.

By far the most successful was the Vickers Viscount which had its origins in the Brabazon Committee's Type IIB specification for a 24-seater medium range airliner powered by four turboprops. As design work progressed, consultation with BEA resulted in an increase in size to 32 seats and the prototype Vickers Type 630 (originally named the Viceroy) flew for the first time on 16 July 1948, powered by four Rolls-Royce RDa1 turboprops. By then BEA had lost interest but the availability of the more powerful RDa3 Dart led Vickers to design a larger 53-seat version known as the Viscount 700. The prototype flew in August 1950, to be followed for an order from BEA for 26 aircraft before the end of the year. By the time that the first Viscounts entered service in 1953, Vickers had won orders from Air France, Aer Lingus, Trans Australian Airlines, and Trans Canada. These were followed by a much sought after sale to an American airline, Capital Airlines, which placed an order for 60 aircraft with deliveries commencing in 1955. In the meantime, one of the first Viscount 700s had participated in the 1953 England-New Zealand air race, painted in BEA colours in an elapsed time of 40hr 45min, a feat which attracted worldwide attention and led to further orders. The Viscount was immensely popular with passengers, having a comfortable pressurised cabin with large oval picture windows, unrivalled standards of quietness and smoothness when compared to contemporary piston-engined airliners, and the ability to cruise at 25,000ft above the worst of the weather – something which had previously made flying an uncomfortable experience. It was no wonder that the world's airlines beat a path to Vickers' door. The 700 series Viscount was powered by four 1,540ehp Rolls-Royce Dart RDa3 500/501 turboprops and normally carried between 40 and 59 passengers. The developed Viscount 800 series first flew in 1956 and, with a fuselage stretched by 46in and the rear pressure bulkhead relocated, could seat between 65 and 70 passengers. It was powered by 1,690ehp Dart RDa5 turboprops and attracted orders from BEA, Transair, Hunting Clan and Eagle Aviation amongst British airlines and among overseas customers gained another American order from Continental Airlines, which bought the Viscount 810 model with more powerful Dart Rda7/1 525s. This was also ordered by Cubana, Lufthansa, Pakistan International, South African Airways, TAP and VASP.

The final Viscount variant was the V843, of which six were ordered by the People's Republic of China, the last of these leaving the Hurn production line in April 1964, by which time a grand total of 444 Viscounts had been built including 151 800/810 series aircraft. This made it the best selling British airliner of all time and the first to gain substantial orders from US airlines. Today there are no Viscounts left in scheduled passenger service but at the time of their introduction over 40 years ago they almost singlehandedly changed the nature of air transport for ever and represented a watershed in the development of the modern airliner. While the Viscount was capturing the short and medium range market around the world, the Bristol Aircraft Company hoped to emulate its success in the long haul market with the Type 175 Britannia, a successor to the failed Brabazon project and conceived on an altogether more modest and practical level. Design on a 48-seater powered by four Bristol Centaurus radial piston engines began in 1947 in response to a specification issued by BOAC. However as work progressed the aircraft grew to seat up to 83 people and the Proteus turboprop became the selected powerplant. The prototype aircraft, now known as the Britannia 101, first flew on 16 August 1952, to be followed by a second aircraft in December 1953. This example followed what was becoming the unfortunately regular practice of British airliner prototypes and was lost following a forced landing on the mudflats of the Severn estuary caused by an uncontrollable fire in one of the engines. Nevertheless, the test programme went ahead and the production Britannia 102 which followed eventually commenced revenue earning operations with BOAC in January 1957, having been delayed for six months because of unexpected problems with compressor icing in the Proteus 705 turboprops. Carrying up to 98 passengers, the Britannias brought new standards of quietness and comfort to BOAC's long haul routes to Africa and the Far East and proved very popular. The original order for 25 aircraft was cut back to 15 as interest passed to an all-cargo and mixed passenger-cargo versions (Series 200 and 250 respectively) although eventually it was the Britannia 300 which was ordered by BOAC in 1955. This had a fuselage stretched to 142ft 3in and was powered by four 4,120ehp Proteus 755 turboprops. Maximum all-up weight rose to 185,000lb and, in its long range guise with additional fuel tanks, it could cover 4,268 miles with a full load of passengers (between 82 and 139 depending on configuration) making it suitable for transatlantic operations. Cruising speed was 357mph and the Series 300 proved attractive to other long haul airlines including Aeronaves de Mexico, Transcontinental SA, Air Charter and Ghana Airways, while the Britannia 310 series with uprated Proteus engines was ordered by BOAC, El Al, Canadian Pacific, Hunting Clan and Cubana. Production of the Britannia ceased in 1960 after only 82 aircraft had been completed, including 20 of the military Britannia 252 for the Royal Air Force. This total was much less than Bristol had hoped for and was partly due to the lengthy development period which meant that when the aircraft was finally entering service, and substantial orders might have been expected, the air transport world was at the threshold of the jet age and the Britannia, whatever its many technical merits, was seen as obsolete. Ironically, the aircraft which started the movement which was to cut the ground from under the world's piston and turboprop long haul airliners was itself British – the famous, yet tragic, de Havilland Comet.

Conceived in answer to yet another Brabazon Committee specification, the de Havilland DH106 Comet was a singularly graceful aircraft, powered initially by four 4,450lb thrust de Havilland Ghost 50 centrifugal flow turbojets. When it first flew, on 27 July 1949, it was light years ahead of any conventional airliner and during its test programme, which proceeded remarkably smoothly with little hint of the disasters ahead, it broke numerous distance records at cruising speeds of around 420kts. The Comet 1 was small by today's standards, carrying between 36 and 44 passengers, and was not capable of transatlantic services. Despite this, by 1951 the Comet was in full production and several aircraft had been delivered to BOAC which began route training flights carrying cargo payloads in January 1952, and inaugurated the world's first scheduled jet service on 2 May 1952 with a flight from London to Johannesburg. The reputation of the British aircraft industry now stood at its highest and orders for the Comet began to roll in. Early customers included Canadian Pacific Airlines, Air France and UTA, while many American airlines were also close to placing orders when a series of tragic, and initially unexplained, accidents resulted in the grounding of the entire Comet fleet.

The first aircraft to be lost was G-ALYV which broke up while climbing out of Calcutta on 2 May 1953; two more aircraft also broke up without warning after taking-off from Rome on 10 January and 8 April 1954. At this stage there was no option but to cease Comet operations and one of the most painstaking accident investigations ever undertaken began. The search to recover the wreckage of G-ALYP, which had crashed into the Mediterranean off Elba, involved the first use of underwater television. Eventually the cause was traced to a failure in the pressure cabin at one of the rear windows, caused by little understood fatigue stresses. The lessons of the Comet disasters were applied to new versions of the aircraft and were generously made available to other manufacturers but it was too late. The Comet lost its world-beating position and the British aircraft industry took decades to recover. A more powerful Comet 2 powered by four Rolls-Royce Avon 502 axial flow engines had flown in February 1952 and offered longer range than its Ghost-engined predecessor but, after modifications to the fuselage structure following the accidents, they were diverted from BOAC to the Royal Air Force who flew them successfully until they were retired in 1967. Further development of the civil airliner, incorporating all the lessons learned from the Rome crashes, started with the stretched 78-seater Comet 3 which flew in July 1954 and led to the definitive Comet 4 with 10,500lb thrust Avon 524 engines and distinctive long range fuel tanks mounted at mid-span on the wing's leading edges. This first flew in April 1958 and on 4 October later that year BOAC finally introduced transatlantic jet passenger services, just three weeks ahead of Pan American with their new Boeing 707s. Britain's other state airline, BEA, also ordered 14 Comet 4Bs, which featured a longer fuselage seating up to 101 passengers and a short span wing without the long range tanks as these were not required for European services. The final Comet variant was the 4C which combined the long fuselage of the Comet 4B with the long range wing of the 4 and 4A. Apart from the two British airlines, the Comet 4 achieved a modest export success and was bought by a number of airlines including Air India, Qantas, Olympic, Aerolineas Argentinas, Kuwait Airways, Middle East Airlines and United Arab Airlines. In all, 74 Comet 4s were built, adding to the 21 Comet 1s, 23 Comet 2s (not all completed) and a single Comet 3 prototype. What might have been if the Comet had lived up to its early promise can only be imagined.

While the Comet was undisputably the world's first jet airliner to see commercial service, it is often forgotten that the next to see service was Russian. The aircraft concerned was the twin-engined swept-wing Tupolev Tu-104, which first flew in 1955 and began regular passenger carrying flights with Aeroflot, the Russian state airline, in September 1956. It was first revealed to western eyes when it made a sensational appearance at London Heathrow carrying Russian officials in March of that year. Its design was based on that of the Tupolev Tu-16 bomber but featured a larger fuselage seating 50 passengers and was powered by

two Mikulin AM-3M turbojets housed in nacelles located at the root of the sharply swept wings. An unusual visual feature was the pair of streamlined cones projecting from the wing trailing edge which housed the main undercarriage units when retracted. The original Tu-104 was rapidly followed by the 70-seater Tu-104A which flew in 1956 and subsequently made several flights establishing world records in height and speed with a payload. In 1959 a stretched 100-seater Tu-104B was introduced onto Aeroflot's routes throughout Russia and Europe. Although regarded as rather crude when compared to subsequent western aircraft, the Tu-104 was a rugged workhorse in the Russian tradition and remained in service in substantial numbers until the end of the 1970s.

Prior to the introduction of the jets, most Russian airliners were adaptations of military transport designs and made little concession to passenger comfort. However a notable exception was the Ilyushin Il-12 and its successor, the Il-14. Although similar in appearance to the contemporary Convair 240/340, the Russian designs were smaller and, lacking pressurisation, were less sophisticated. The Il-12 was powered by a pair of 1,650hp ASh-82FN radial engines, had a modern appearance with a tricycle undercarriage and could carry up to 27 passengers. It first flew in early 1946 and over 3,000 had been built by 1953 when it was succeeded on the production line by the Il-14. This had more powerful 1,900hp ASh-82T radials and featured various aerodynamic improvements, the most noticeable being a new large squared-off tail fin. The final Russian version was the Il-14M which appeared in 1956 and could carry up to 32 passengers. The type was also produced in East Germany and Czechoslovakia, the latter also building an improved model under the designation Avia 14. Around 7,000 Il-12s and 14s are believed to have been produced, making it the most prolific airliner apart from the Douglas DC-3.

The next European jet airliner came from France which, in the early postwar years, produced a few interesting but commercially unsuccessful airliners. One of the first was the four-engined SE161 Languedoc which flew in September 1945 – although in fact it was an updated version of the Marcel Bloch MB161 which had flown in 1939 but whose development had virtually halted during the war. Powered by Pratt & Whitney R-1830-S1G3-G radials, the Languedoc carried 33 passengers in a rather narrow fuselage and maximum range with this payload was only 630 miles. Some 100 were built. A more novel design was the Breguet Br761 Deux Ponts which flew in 1949 and was easily distinguished by its deep double-deck fuselage. The original Gnome Rhône radial engines were replaced by four 2,020hp Pratt & Whitney R-2800-B31 engines and the improved Br763 (known as the Provence) entered service with Air France in 1953 carrying 59 passengers on the upper deck and a further 48 on the lower deck. As a freighter, the Deux Ponts/Provence could carry 11 tons of cargo and six of the 12 aircraft delivered to Air France were taken over by the Armée de l'Air in 1964. A total of 19 of these large Breguets was built and one of the early Br761s was briefly evaluated as a potential car ferry by Silver City Airways in the early 1950s.

The Comet will always be remembered as the progenitor of the world's jet airliner services – and for the crashes, and the subsequent accident investigation, that dealt such a blow to the aircraft's commercial success. The Comet 4 derived from the first major stretch of the basic de Havilland DH106 airframe – the Comet 3, designed for transatlantic operations. The Comet 4 incorporated all the findings of the 1954 accident reports and differed little from the Mk 3 except for accommodation for more passengers, improved engines and a higher weight. The 4B (an example is shown here) first flew on 27 June 1959 and BEA began 4B services between London and Moscow early in 1960. The 4C was the final version of the Comet, combining the 4B's long fuselage with the 4's big wing, giving a max cruising speed of 535mph and a 4,310-mile range. Altogether 74 Comet 4/4A/4B/ 4C variants were built, the two unsold 4C airframes being rebuilt into the Nimrod prototypes.

However, the aircraft which was to establish the French aircraft industry as a major force in the airliner market was the revolutionary Sud Ouest Caravelle twin-engined jet, the first to be designed from the start as a short to medium range airliner. The specification which eventually led to the Caravelle was issued in 1951 and the SE210 design was selected for development. The most interesting aspect of this project was the positioning of the two Rolls-Royce Avon jet engines which were mounted on either side of the rear fuselage, an arrangement subsequently to be copied and adopted by numerous other manufacturers and designers. The smooth and graceful looking Caravelle prototype flew in 1955 and subsequently entered airline service with Air France in 1959, closely followed by SAS, the first of many export customers. The early Caravelles carried up to 99 passengers although 64-70 was a more typical payload. A total of 32 Caravelle 1/1As was built, followed by a further 78 Caravelle IIIs with uprated Avon RA29/3 Mk 527 engines. Next came a further 109 Caravelle VIs with even more powerful engines; customers included United Airlines and Sabena, and these were the last of the Avon-engined variants to be delivered. With a cruising speed of 425kts, the Caravelle VI could carry a maximum payload over a range of 1,430 miles with reserves. Continued production now centred on the Caravelle 10B which was powered by 14,000lb thrust Pratt & Whitney JT8D-1 turbofans, this version making its maiden flight in 1964, while the final production version was the Caravelle 12 which was the first to have a fuselage stretch, increasing passenger capacity to a maximum of 140. The last of 282 Caravelles to be built was a Caravelle 12 delivered to Sterling Airways of Denmark in 1972. The Caravelle was a fine aircraft and sold in substantial numbers to prestige customers including Alitalia, Finnair and Iberia, apart from those already mentioned; in doing so it achieved the commercial success so cruelly denied to the ill fated Comet.

1960s

Although the efforts and achievements of the British engineers in developing the first operational jet and turboprop airliners cannot be denied, it was American industry which eventually ushered in the era of mass air transport with its first generation of large jet airliners which rapidly reached maturity in the 1960s. In the piston-engined era the Douglas Aircraft Company had reigned supreme but its pre-eminence was on the verge of being lost for ever when Pan American introduced its new four-engined swept-wing Boeing 707 airliner in 1958. In fact the prototype of this aircraft, originally designated the Model 367-80, had flown as far back as July 1954 but, with modifications, the type first entered production as the KC-135 military transport and aerial tanker to support Strategic Air Command's fleet of Boeing-built Stratojet and Stratofortress bombers. Pan American placed an order for 29 Boeing 707s in October 1955 and the basic design was refined in the light of experience with the military versions. Initial examples of the civil 707 delivered to Pan Am early in 1958 were 707-120s, powered by four 13,000lb thrust Pratt & Whitney JT3C turbojets, and could carry up to 179 passengers. This version was basically intended for US transcontinental services and was not really suitable for transatlantic services, suffering severe payload restrictions and often requiring refuelling stops at Gander, Shannon and Prestwick when used on this route. However competition from BOAC with its new Comet 4s forced Pan Am to start such services with the 707-120 on 26 October 1958. Nevertheless, the 707 introduced a new era of airline travel, carrying much greater numbers of passengers than the Comet, these being accommodated in a new six-abreast seating configuration which is now virtually standard in most medium range and many long haul airliners.

The true long range version of the 707 was the 707-320 or 707-420 which were respectively powered by either four 15,800lb thrust JT4A or 16,500lb thrust Rolls-Royce Conway 505 engines. Dubbed the Boeing 707 Intercontinental, both of these variants featured a lengthened fuselage seating up to 189 passengers, increased all-up weight and fuel capacity, increased wingspan and other aerodynamic refinements including a taller fin and ventra strake. With these improvements, the JT4A-powered Intercontinental had a range of 4,300 miles with a full load and cruised at up to 480kts. The 707-320 entered service with Pan Am at the end of 1959 and BOAC introduced its 707-420s in May 1960. An improved B model of all versions was produced in 1962 and featured a redesigned wing with greater area and improved high lift devices, and also incorporated thrust reversers on the JT3D-3 turbofans. The final variant was the 707-300C (Convertible) which had a 7ft by 11ft cargo door on the left side of the forward fuselage and a strengthened main deck floor to allow various combinations of freight and passengers to be carried.

In 1959 Boeing flew the first of a lightweight short range version of the basic design known as the Boeing 720. Although externally almost indistinguishable from the 707, the new aircraft was regarded as a separate aircraft type and could carry up to 149 passengers on high density short range routes. Initial customers were United and Eastern Airlines and a total of 154 was built. The 707 (and its 720 derivative) established Boeing as a major manufacturer of jet airliners and no fewer than 916 civil 707s were delivered between 1958 and 1982 when the last example was rolled out at Seattle, although many hundreds of the military version were also built and the basic airframe remained in production until 1993 when the last E-3 Sentry (an AEW version of the 707) was delivered to the RAF.

Douglas did not take the Boeing challenge lying down and confidently expected its rival DC-8 design would be a best seller. Development of the new four-engined jet airliner lagged behind the 707 although it received a great boost in 1955 when Pan Am, obviously hedging its bets, ordered 20 DC-8s at the same time as it placed a similar order for 707s. The prototype DC-8 did not fly until 30 May 1958, powered by four Pratt & Whitney JT3C turbojets. In outline it was similar to the 707 in that it carried the engines in pods mounted under the sharply swept wing and carried a similar number of passengers, 117-189 depending on the configuration. The initial model was the DC-8 Series 10, immediately followed by the Series 20 version which had more powerful JT4As for improved take-off performance. Both of these were intended for domestic operations and the first intercontinental version was the JT4A-powered Series 30 which entered service on transatlantic routes with KLM and Pan American in 1960, while the Rolls-Royce Conway-powered Series 40 was ordered by TCA/Air Canada, Alitalia and Canadian Pacific. Also in 1960, the first Series 50 flew, introducing the new JT3D turbofan engine, offering a significant advance in fuel economy and allowing much greater range. For example, with a take-off weight of 325,000lb, the ultimate Series 55 could fly over 700 miles further than the comparable Series 33.

The Boeing 707 was one of the mileposts of aviation history. Stemming from a military requirement which produced the KC-135 tanker, not only were over 800 of all military variants built but, in addition, 1,009 Boeing 707s of all types were built, the main variants being the -320 and 720. The different models vary considerably in size and performance: the first production 707-120 – for Pan Am which had ordered 20 aircraft in 1955 – first flew on 20 December 1957 having 13,500lb st Pratt & Whitney JT3C-6 turbojets. The -320 first flew on 11 January 1959, had a larger span by 15ft, and in its -320C version had 18,000lb st P&W JT3D-3B turbofans and could carry nearly twice the payload, at 83,447lb.

Illustrated is OD-AGV, a 707-347C of Middle East Airlines, seen in May 1987; it is still flying today.

Despite a sparkling performance, the standard DC-8 was a poor seller compared with the Boeing 707 and only 294 were sold. However, the potential of the new generation of turbofans was fully realised in the substantially improved Series 60 aircraft which was produced in three versions. The DC-8-61 appeared in 1966 and the most obvious difference was a massive 36ft 8in stretch of the fuselage, which could now seat up to 259 passengers. The DC-8-62, which flew in the following year, had a more modest 6ft 8in stretch but with aerodynamic improvements and greater fuel capacity could carry up to 189 passengers over ranges in excess of 5,000 miles. The final DC-8-63 took to the air in 1967 and combined the long fuselage of the Series 61 with the improvements of the Series 62 to produce an outstandingly successful long range high capacity airliner. Some 262 Series 60 aircraft were sold and Douglas only stopped production in 1972 because it was concerned that this success would affect sales of the much larger DC-10 then being introduced. Although beaten by the 707 in many respects, the DC-8 did have one major claim to fame – it was the first civil airliner to exceed the speed of sound, this amazing milestone being achieved in shallow dive by a DC-8-53 under test in the spring of 1962.

The obvious merit of the DC-8 Series 60 airframe led to a rejuvenation of the design in 1977 when a company named Cammacorp was set up to remanufacture these aircraft and fit them with new 22,000lb thrust CFM56 high bypass ratio turbofans. In this guise the Series 61,62 and 63 models became the Series 71,72 and 73. Some 110 aircraft were eventually converted and served with United Airlines, Delta, Air Canada and UTA among others. Many DC-8s of all variants were built as, or converted to, freighter configuration and it is these which mostly survive today, accounting for the majority of the 256 DC-8s still flying.

A third US contender in the race to produce the new breed of large jet airliners was Convair, which had achieved much success with its small Convair Liners. However its venture into the jet market is generally regarded as something of a disaster. In order not to compete head on with Boeing and Douglas, Convair designed a smaller four-engined aircraft with the accent very much on high speed cruise performance. Development started in 1956 and the prototype of the Convair 880 took to the air on 27 January 1959 powered by four 11,200lb thrust General Electric CJ805 turbojets which endowed the aircraft with a maximum speed of 535kts although more typical cruising speed was 485kts, still faster than its rivals. A slim fuselage seated between 88 and 110 passengers in five abreast seating, but despite orders from TWA and Delta, the Convair 880 achieved limited success with only 65 produced. A larger version, the Convair 990, was produced in 1961 and this could seat up to 106 passengers but aerodynamic problems encountered in the test programme showed serious deficiencies in handling and performance characteristics. The 990 featured a new wing which carried four streamlined fairings on the trailing edge which were intended to reduce drag and increase cruising speeds. Customers included American Airlines, Swissair, SAS, Garuda Indonesian and Varig but again sales success was limited and only 37 were delivered.

Across the Atlantic, Britain attempted to recover ground lost by the problems experienced by the Comet. Starting in 1956, Vickers Armstrong began development of a four-engined jet airliner, initially aimed at meeting BOAC's requirements for an aircraft to serve its routes to Africa and the Far East. The final design was for a handsome aircraft with four Rolls-Royce Conway turbofans mounted in pairs on either side of the rear fuselage. By the time the prototype VC-10 flew in June 1962, its specification had been improved to allow transatlantic operations carrying up to 150 passengers. When it entered service with BOAC in 1964 it was rapturously received by both passengers and pilots alike. The rear-mounted engines made for a quiet cabin and the clean wing contributed to the aircraft's delightful handling characteristics. The stretched Super VC-10, which could seat up to 174 passengers, flew in 1964 and could carry a maximum payload over 4,720 miles at a cruising speed of 475kts. Despite the obvious merits of the VC-10, it was not able to overcome the marketing advantage of the American giants and only 32 VC-10s and 22 Super VC-10s were sold, these totals including 14 delivered to the RAF. Apart from BOAC, other customers were Ghana Airways, British United Airways and East African Airlines. British Airways operated its Super VC-10s until 1981 and most of its aircraft were subsequently converted to military tankers.

In the meantime Russia also entered the field with a design which bore a remarkable similarity to the British VC-10 – the Ilyushin Il-62. This first flew in January 1963 and during the test programme several aerodynamic modifications were made and the original Lyulka AL-7 turbojets were replaced by 23,150lb thrust Kuznetsov NK-8 turbofans. Accommodation ranged from 85 passengers with sleeping couches on long range intercontinental routes to 186 seats in a high density layout. With a monopoly of the eastern bloc market, the Il-62 was produced in greater numbers than the VC-10, over 100 being delivered to Aeroflot while others were sold to Czechoslovak State Airlines (CSA), Interflug, LOT, and Tarom. An improved Il-62M entered service in 1974 powered by four 25,350lb thrust Soloviev D-30KU turbofans which allowed higher gross operating weights and the carriage of more fuel to improve payload/range performance. This version continued in production into the 1980s and today over 160 Il-62/62M aircraft remain in service.

Interestingly, the original Il-62 replaced the earlier and unique Tupolev Tu-114 which, at the time of its first flight in 1957, was the world's largest airliner and the only swept-wing turboprop airliner ever to enter service. Based on the Tupolev Tu-20/Tu-95 bomber (better known under its NATO codename 'Bear'), the Tu-114 could seat up to 220 passengers although the standard mixed class layout seated 170 while only 120 were carried on long range intercontinental flights. Despite being a turboprop, the Russian monster cruised at around 410kts, only slightly slower than the contemporary Comet and Boeing 707, and was capable of very long distance flights – such as from Moscow to Cuba non-stop.

While the four-engined jet was becoming standard for long haul services, the turboprop was still considered most suitable for short and medium range high density routes and Britain, America and Russia all produced very similar aircraft to meet this requirement. In Britain, Vickers attempted to capitalise on its success with the Viscount by producing a larger design powered by four 5,545ehp Rolls-Royce Tyne turboprops which could carry up to 140 passengers in a one class layout. Known as the Vanguard, this aircraft flew in 1959 after six years of design and development and entered service with BEA at the end of 1960. Production totalled 44 aircraft of which 20 went to BEA and 23 to Trans Canada Airline but, despite the aircraft's excellent performance and operating economics, no further orders were forthcoming as new jet designs were now becoming available. One design feature of the

For many the Vickers (BAC) VC-10 and its stretched version, the Super VC-10, represented Britain's best chance to compete with the American giants in the postwar civil aviation market. Designed for BOAC 'hot and high' use, this second generation jet was the first long-haul aircraft to see a rear-engined configuration. Unfortunately, BOAC reduced its initial order for 30 Supers, eventually – after a good deal of political argy-bargy – buying more 707-320Cs, and the chance had gone. Despite great public appeal and excellent performances, the VC-10 would soldier on into the 1980s as an RAF tanker; transatlantic traffic would travel by Boeing, Douglas or Lockheed aircraft.

Vanguard was the fuselage, which had a deep 'double bubble' profile which permitted the carriage of a considerable amount of freight and cargo in the lower holds. This facility resulted in many redundant passenger aircraft being converted to an all-cargo configuration and in this guise they were operated by BEA and British Airways under the name Merchantman, serving in this role until 1980. Some of these were taken over by Air Bridge carriers which later became Hunting Cargo Airlines; Hunting would retire the last airworthy Vanguard/Merchantman in 1996 when it was delivered, by air, to the Brooklands Aviation Museum where it can be seen today.

The American equivalent of the Vanguard was the Lockheed L188 Electra. Produced in response to an American Airlines' specification for an aircraft suitable for use on short/medium range US domestic routes, the Electra was powered by four 3,750ehp Allison 501-D13A turboprops, similar to those which powered the Lockheed Hercules military transports. Following its first flight in December 1957, the Electra entered airline service with Eastern and American Airlines in January 1959. At the time of its initial flight, Lockheed held orders for 144 aircraft but a series of fatal accidents dented sales prospects and the final total was 170, still much better than the British Vanguard; the design lives on today as a basis for the Lockheed P-3 Orion maritime patrol aircraft which is still in production.

Russia appeared to produce another 'copycat' design when the Ilyushin Il-18 was unveiled to western eyes in mid-1957. In fact the design was completely original and was unusual amongst Russian airliners of the period in that it was intended from the outset as a commercial aircraft and was not adapted from any military aircraft. Standard production Il-18s were powered by 4,000ehp Ivchenko AI-20 turboprops and could carry around 84 passengers. Later developments could accommodate up to 122 passengers and were powered by more powerful AI-20M engines. In contrast to its western equivalents, the Il-18 enjoyed a long production life and over 800 were built with many still in service today.

By the mid-1950s the piston-engined airliner was seen as outdated and, apart from small commuter types, almost all future designs incorporated jet or turboprop powerplants. Several successful small turboprop airliners had their origins at this time. The best known of these was the work of the famous Dutch designer, Fokker, who produced the prototype 32-seater pressurised Fokker F27 Friendship in 1955. This was powered by two Rolls-Royce Dart turboprops and was an immediate success although production versions featured a lengthened fuselage to seat up to 40 passengers. Entering service with Aer Lingus in 1958, the Friendship also quickly penetrated the US market and West Coast Airlines received its first aircraft in the same year. The basic soundness of the popular Friendship is illustrated by the fact that it remained in production until 1987 when the last of 786 aircraft was delivered, a Series 600 which could seat up to 56 passengers and was powered by two 2,140shp Rolls-Royce Dart RDa7 engines. This total includes 206 aircraft produced in America between 1958 and 1968 by Fairchild, 78 of these being known as Fairchild FH-227s which were a longer-fuselaged version based on the parent company's F-27 Mk 500. Over 280 Fokker and Fairchild-produced Friendships remain in service today, as well as several more flown by various military air arms; these figures contrast starkly with lack of success achieved by the rival Handley Page Herald produced in Britain. This aircraft originally flew in 1955 but was powered by four 850hp piston engines. Faced with competition from Fokker, the British design was revised to a twin turboprop configuration using the ubiquitous Rolls-Royce Dart, and flew in this guise in 1958. Despite having a similar performance to its Dutch rival, only 50 Heralds had been sold by the time that Handley Page went into liquidation in 1970 and only a handful remain in service today.

A much more successful British product was the Hawker Siddeley 748 (originally the Avro 748). Yet another aircraft to be powered by Rolls-Royce Darts, the 748 adopted a rugged low wing design and could seat up to 48 passengers in its original Series 1 configuration: the subsequent Series 2 could accommodate up 52. The 748 first flew in 1960 and no fewer

While so many manufacturers were looking to the glamorous longer-haul markets, Fokker identified the short-range replacement for the C-47 as its market for the 1950s. The result was the Fokker F27 Friendship, which was built from the late 1950s until 1986: nearly 800 aircraft in total, of which 206 were built under licence by Fairchild (later Fairchild Hiller) in the USA – 128 F-27s and 78 of the stretched FH-227s. This classic short-range twin turboprop received Dutch government backing and first flew in 1955 with seats for 28 passengers – the stretched versions could carry 60. There were many interesting variants, including the F27M Troopship, a night airmail version for the French postal services, the F-27B Freightship and the F27MPA Maritime for coastal patrol duties. This Oceanair Fairchild F-27F is seen at San Juan, Puerto Rico, in January 1982.

than 382 were produced between then and 1988, including 89 assembled under licence by HAL in India. It was one of the first civil airliners to have what was termed 'a fail safe structure' whereby the failure of any structural component would not result in the failure of major components leading to the loss of the aircraft. Such a philosophy is now universally applied to aircraft design but it was a major advance at the time.

Once again Russian designers came up with a similar solution to their western counterparts when they produced the Antonov An-24 in 1960. This twin-engined high-wing turboprop could carry up to 50 passengers and was produced in great numbers for both military and commercial purposes. Over 1,100 An-24s were built and as well as being widely used throughout the eastern bloc, it was also sold to other customers including Egyptair, Air Mali, CAAC, Cubana and Iraqi Airways. The basic design was developed in several variants including the An-26 with a rear loading ramp, the An-30 with a redesigned forward fuselage and the An-32 with 5,180ehp Ivchenko AI-20M engines. Including these versions, over 1,500 Antonov twin turboprops remain in service and, with the improvement in east/west relationships, they are becoming an increasingly common sight at all the world's airports.

Although there was obviously a market for smaller turboprops such as the Fokker Friendship and the HS748, by the early 1960s airlines were turning to jet designs for anything carrying more than 100 passengers and the manufacturers had plenty of options on their drawing boards. The first to fly was the British DH121 Trident, powered by three 9,850lb thrust Rolls-Royce RB163 Spey turbofans, which took to the air in January 1962. Prior to this, the famous de Havilland name was lost in a process of rationalisation and the Trident was subsequently produced under the Hawker Siddeley label. Unfortunately, the original Trident 1 was closely tailored to a BEA specification and was too small for most other airlines. Attempts to improve the type's marketability resulted in the uprated Trident 1E with an increased wingspan and seating for 115 passengers, and the Trident 2E with more powerful engines. The 2E was the first airliner in the world to be certified for fully automatic landings in poor weather conditions – a major step forward in improving the reliability of commercial air services, as well as offering a significant improvement in safety standards. The ultimate Trident was the 3B, a short range high density version carrying up to 180 passengers. It was actually a four-engined aircraft as it incorporated a 5,250lb thrust RB168 turbojet in the base of the tailfin. This extra engine was used as a booster for take-off and was shut down in cruising flight. Despite all this development, the Trident's main customer remained BEA, although a few were sold to other airlines including Kuwait Airways, Iraqi Airlines, Pakistan International, Channel Airways, Air Ceylon and CAAC. Total production of all versions was 117 aircraft of which no fewer than 65 were for BEA.

One reason for the Trident's relative lack of success was the fact that a rival design appeared on the other side of the Atlantic in the shape of the Boeing 727, also a medium range three-engined jet. Although flying over a year later than the Trident, on 9 February 1963, the Boeing 727 could seat up to 139 passengers and carry them up to 1,700 miles at a cruising speed of up to 480kts. This combination of range and payload could not be matched by the smaller Trident and the American manufacturer swept the board, turning the 727 into the best selling jet airliner of its day with 1,831 aircraft delivered up to 1984 when production ceased. Apart from its performance, the 727 was also attractive to passengers and airlines as it retained the same fuselage cross-section and standards of comfort as the larger Boeing 707. The original Boeing 727-100, powered by three 14,000lb thrust Pratt & Whitney JT8D turbofans, was produced in passenger and combi versions but was replaced by the lengthened 727-200 in 1967. With a 20ft increase in fuselage length, the 727-200 could seat up to 189 passengers and more powerful JT8Ds allowed an increase in range to 2,500 miles with full payload. In 1972 Boeing produced the 727-200 Advanced, which allowed operation at higher gross weights and had a number of other improvements.

Yet again, Russian designers came up with a similar design, although this was to a slightly later timescale than the Trident and 727, the Tupolev Tu-154 not making its maiden flight until October 1968 since when 800 have been produced. The type did not enter full scale service with Aeroflot until 1972 but since then it has been widely adopted by former Russian states and many Asian and East European operators. Naturally there has been considerable development of the basic design and the current production version is the Tu-154M powered by three 23,380lb thrust Soloviev D-30KU turbofans. This can carry up to 180 passengers in six abreast seating.

While the tri-jets were battling for orders, a market was also developing for smaller twin-engined jet airliners and, once again, the British led the way with the BAC 1-11 which flew first in August 1963. The British Aircraft Corporation had been formed in 1960 by the merger of several British aerospace companies including Vickers and Hunting Aircraft and the BAC 1-11 was based on a Hunting project. In prototype form the BAC 1-11 Series 100 was a 65-seater but the first production versions, delivered to British United in 1965, had grown to a gross weight of 73,500lb and could seat up to 79 passengers. Unfortunately the flight test programme was severely disrupted by the loss of the prototype in a tragic crash which killed all seven people on board. Investigation showed that the accident was caused by the onset of a deep stall condition from which the aircraft could not recover, this set of circumstances being related to the T-tail configuration adopted for the aircraft. Several modifications were incorporated to prevent a repeat of this and the lessons learned were passed on to US manufacturers such as Boeing and Douglas who were also developing T-tailed designs. BAC had high hopes for the 1-11 which promised to emulate the success of the earlier Viscount; substantial orders were received from US airlines including Braniff, Mohawk and American. Production variants were the Series 200, 300 and 400, each featuring various improvements and different versions of the Rolls-Royce RB163 Spey turbofan but these all retained the same fuselage. The major development was the Series 500, ordered by BEA, which had a lengthened fuselage and increased wingspan as well as uprated engines. It first flew in 1967, initially designed to carry 97 passengers; in fact the BAC 1-11-500 was eventually certificated to carry a maximum of 119. The final production variant was the Series 475 which had the original fuselage married to the extended wing and more powerful engines of the Series 500. British production of the BAC 1-11 totalled 232 up to 1982 when production was transferred to Romania where the aircraft continued to be built, as the Rombac 111, from kits supplied by BAC/British Aerospace. While this made it the most successful British jet airliner at that time, sales did not reach the hoped for levels and were totally eclipsed by two very significant aircraft which were to appear in the US – the Douglas DC-9 and the Boeing 737.

The first of these to fly was the DC-9, which took the air at Long Beach, California, on 25 February 1965, almost two years after the BAC 1-11, and was destined to become the most successful of all the Douglas commercial jets with developed versions still in production today. The initial variant, delivered to Delta Airlines, was the DC-9 Series 10 which was powered by two 12,000lb thrust Pratt & Whitney JT8D turbofans and could carry up to 90 passengers. However the main production variant was the DC-9 Series 30 which entered service with Eastern Airlines in February 1967. It had a 15ft increase in fuselage length to allow up to 115 passengers to be carried, a 4ft increase in wingspan, uprated JT8D engines and maximum weight increased from 77,000lb to 98,000lb. Subsequent developments included the Series 40 for SAS in 1967, with an additional 6ft 2in fuselage stretch to raise capacity to 125 passengers, and the Series 50 for Swissair in 1974 with yet a further stretch to accommodate 139 passengers. Each of these versions had more powerful JT8D engines and maximum weight rose to 121,000lb. The flexibility of the basic design, which allowed continual growth, was a major factor in its success and over 50 airlines eventually bought DC-9s. No fewer than 976 were produced, 584 of these being DC-9-30s.

Almost unbelievably, Douglas' success with the DC-9 was to pale in comparison with the sales record of the next twin-jet airliner to fly, the staggeringly successful Boeing 737. Being heavily committed to the earlier 707 and 727 models, Boeing was slow to enter the market for a small twin-jet airliner and the first 737-100 did not fly until 7 April 1967 – in retrospect, one of the most significant dates in airliner history. At the time, many observers thought that Boeing had made a major mistake in producing the 737 as the market already seemed saturated with the Caravelle, BAC 1-11 and the already successful DC-9. Indeed only a few 737-100s were built, the main customer being Lufthansa, before production switched to the 737-200 which had a slightly longer fuselage seating up to 130 passengers. It was powered by two 15,500lb thrust Pratt & Whitney JT8D-9A turbofans which, unusually given the configuration adopted by all the rival designs, were mounted under the wing. Another significant point of difference was the fuselage, which was again of the same cross-section as the 707 (and the 727) permitting six abreast seating compared to the five abreast arrangement of the DC-9 and BAC 1-11. This did give the 737 a rather tubby appearance leading to its well known nickname of FLUFF (Fat Little Ugly Fellow!). In parallel with the earlier Boeing 727, an Advanced model of the 737 was produced in 1971 and through the use of aerodynamic

The BAC 1-11 originated from a Hunting Aircraft project and was the first major civil programme undertaken by the British Aircraft Corporation. Initially successful – a total of 232 was built in the UK (with hopes for 80 licence-built in Romania) a very respectable figure – the 1-11 lost out in the head-to-head battle with the Boeing 737 and Douglas DC-9, two of the most successful short/medium haul airliners ever with over 2,500 and nearly 1,000 sales respectively. This Dan Air 1-11-207, G-ATVH, is pictured in September 1985.

refinements, increased all-up weight and fuel capacity, the range with 115 passengers rose from 2,136 miles to 2,370 miles. British Airways was a major customer for this version, placing orders for no fewer than 44 aircraft which were delivered between 1981 and 1985, replacing the British-built Tridents. Other improvements to the 737 were added progressively as the production figures rose at a staggering rate until 1,144 of these early 737s had been produced when the last Series 200 was completed in 1988.

The Soviet equivalent of the DC-9 and BAC 1-11 was the Tupolev Tu-134, an 84-seater with a T-tailed rear-engined configuration which first flew in 1962. Over 700 were subsequently completed, of which around 400 still remain in service. However its performance was inferior to its western counterparts, particularly in respect of range, and it was not stretched or developed to the same extent. Another contemporary was the French-built Dassault Breguet Mercure, a Boeing 737 lookalike which flew in 1971 and entered service with Air Inter, its only customer, in 1974. Only 11 production aircraft were built and plans to produce an enlarged Mercure 200 in conjunction with McDonnell Douglas did not reach fruition. The surviving Mercures were withdrawn from service in 1994-95 – an expensive manifestation of Gallic pride!

Despite the failure of the Mercure, in the early 1970s the French (and British) aerospace industry appeared to be on the verge of a runaway success to which the Americans had no answer. Over the previous decade the two countries had collaborated to design, build and fly the world's first successful supersonic airliner, the Concorde, and the world's airlines were queuing up to buy it. The origins of the Concorde programme went back as far as 1955 when British engineers began to investigate the problems associated with a supersonic commercial aircraft and their ideas eventually crystallised around the Bristol 223, a four-engined delta-winged aircraft capable of carrying 110 passengers from London to New York. In the meantime, the French aerospace industry had come up with a very similar design known as the Super Caravelle and it made both commercial and political sense to set up a formal collaborative programme which was inaugurated in 1962. While BAC and Aérospatiale collaborated on the airframe, engine design and development was shared by Rolls-Royce and SNECMA. In view of the many technological advances involved attaining safe supersonic commercial flight, it was decided to produce two prototypes (001 and 002), to be followed by two pre-production aircraft (01 and 02). The very first flight of 001 was at Toulouse on 2 March 1969, followed by 002 at Filton on 9 April 1969, 01 at Toulouse on 17 December 1971 and, finally, 02 at Filton on 10 January 1973. The two pre-production aircraft were

The McDonnell Douglas DC-9 family – including the MD-80 and MD-90 – has sold over 2,000 units since the first DC-9 flight on 25 February 1965. Built at Long Beach, California, it was the last civil aircraft designed by Douglas before the merger with McDonnell in 1967. Over 50 million flying hours, over three billion passengers carried, more than 120 airline customers – this is success in global terms. Originally planned as a scaled down DC-8, the success of the BAC 1-11 made Douglas look again at the market requirements and so the DC-9 was born. This is a DC-9-32, EC-BIK, and was new to Iberia on 14 September 1967, the 164th production aircraft. Named Castillo de Guanapay *it is still in service with Aviaco.*

slightly larger than the prototypes and incorporated various refinements as a result of the early test programme. They were powered by four 38,050lb Rolls Royce/SNECMA Olympus 593 turbojets fitted with reheat for acceleration to the aircraft's Mach 2.0 (1,176kts) cruising speed. Concorde proved to be a resounding technical success, an amazing outcome considering the formidable obstacles to be overcome. Even today, after over 20 years of airline service, the aircraft has an enviable safety record. As the test programme got underway, the world's airlines rushed to order their Concordes and at one time the builders held orders and options for over 70 aircraft from such blue chip customers as BOAC, Air France, Pan American, TWA, United and American Airlines, Lufthansa, Air Canada, Japan Airlines and many others. However two factors eventually caused most of these orders to melt away leaving only Air France and BOAC/British Airways as the final customers. These were the massive increase in fuel prices as a result of the 1973 Arab-Israeli war and the rise of the environmental lobby which effectively prevented supersonic flight on overland routes. Neither of these factors were foreseen when the programme began but the outcome was that only 14 production Concordes were built, seven each for Air France and British Airways, and the last was delivered in 1979.

Commercial services began in 1976, since when the few Concordes flying have established a reputation which completely belies the small size of the fleet. With a luxury premium service, and taking only three hours to fly from London or Paris to New York, Concorde is now the only acceptable way for the rich, famous and powerful to travel, although ordinary mortals have the opportunity to sample supersonic flight on one of the many charter flights. In an era when almost everybody has flown and air travel is accepted as part of everyday life, Concorde is the one airliner which still makes people stop and stare whenever it flies past, a shining example of the abilities of the British and French designers, engineers and craftsmen who combined to put it into the air.

In fact it was not entirely true to say that Concorde had no rival, as history records that the first supersonic airliner to fly was the Russian Tupolev Tu-144 which bore more than a coincidental resemblance to Concorde and had its maiden flight on 31 December 1968, over two months before Concorde. However, although it achieved supersonic flight in June 1969, the Tu-144 was not suitable for commercial use in its original form and underwent three years of testing and substantial modification before a definitive version appeared at the Paris Air Show in 1973. One obvious change was the addition of retractable canard aerofoils behind the flightdeck to improve low speed handling. The highly reported disintegration of 'Concordski' at the air show damaged its prospects considerably, although recent evidence shows that the accident may have been caused not by technical problems but outside events. In its final form it was slightly larger than Concorde with accommodation for up to 140 passengers and was also slightly faster, cruising at Mach 2.2. Only a few Tu-144s were built, entering service with Aeroflot in 1976; services were suspended in 1978 following a fatal crash near Moscow earlier that year. Since then the aircraft have seen little use and were eventually retired and placed in storage, although at least one airframe has had a new lease of life, being restored to airworthy condition in 1996 for use in a joint Russian American test programme to provide data for a projected new supersonic airliner which may enter service around 2015.

1970s

While speed had always been a major factor in air transport and historically manufacturers have attempted to build an airliner which was faster than that of their competitors, the coming of the jet airliner had put everybody on an equal footing as aerodynamic considerations effectively meant that all airliners had an economic cruising speed of around 450kts. Higher speeds could only be achieved by consuming considerably more fuel and by building technologically advanced, and therefore expensive, aircraft such as Concorde. While Europe went down this avenue, the American aerospace industry took a different view and concentrated on developing a new range of very large airliners which offered considerably reduced seat/mile operating costs: in doing so they finally ushered in the era of true mass air travel.

The first steps had already been taken by McDonnell Douglas (formed in 1967 by the mergers of McDonnell and the Douglas Aircraft Company) when it produced the stretched Series 60 versions of the DC-8 which could carry up to 250 passengers. Spurred on by this development, Boeing investigated a similar version of the 707 but eventually decided on a new design which, while still retaining the basic four-engined swept-wing layout of the earlier aircraft, was 80ft longer and would carry three times as many passengers in a single-deck fuselage configured with eight or ten abreast seating. The new aircraft was given the Model number 747 but soon became known as the Jumbo Jet because of its massive size, dwarfing anything which had gone before. The 747 used much of the technology which Boeing had developed when competing, unsuccessfully, for the USAF C-5 contract which was eventually won by the Lockheed Galaxy. This included the use of the new generation of big turbofans which gave power ratings in excess of 40,000lb thrust, the early 747s being powered by four Pratt & Whitney JT9D-1 turbofans initially rated at 41,000lb thrust. This was later increased to 45,000lb thrust in the JT9D-3DW version which permitted a take-off weight of up to 738,000lb, more than twice that of a fully loaded Boeing 707-320C. Passenger capacity varied from around 350 in a typical mixed class layout to almost 500 in a high density configuration while, in addition, up to 16 tonnes of cargo could be carried in the capacious underfloor holds.

It was one thing to design and build such an aircraft, but quite another to persuade airlines that a market existed for such a giant. In the end a breakthrough was achieved when the president of Pan American, Juan Trippe, made a personal leap of faith and ordered no fewer than 25 Boeing 747s in August 1966. After that the programme gathered momentum and the epoch making first flight took place at Boeing's Everett airfield on 9 February 1969, ushering in a new era of air transport. Pan American began commercial operations in January 1970 followed by TWA the next month, while Lufthansa was the first European airline to begin services, in April 1970. Even while the prototypes were under construction, Boeing had plans to develop and improve the basic design and new variants quickly followed the first flight. The original 747-100 was succeeded by the long range 747-200 which also offered customer airlines a choice of three powerplants, the 48,750lb thrust Pratt & Whitney JT9D-7AW, General Electric CF6-50E (53,000lb thrust) or Rolls-Royce RB211-524B (50,100lb thrust). Gross weight rose to 833,000lb to allow more fuel to be carried and the first 747-200 flew in October 1970. Subsequently the original Series 100 was offered in 1973 as the 100SR, optimised for short range high density routes, and as the 100B with higher gross weight and a choice of powerplants in 1978.

In a reversal of the normal process of stretching designs, Boeing offered a short fuselage version known as the 747SP (Special Performance) which was intended for ultra long range, up to 8,000-mile, services with a reduced passenger load, although only a few of these were built as performance improvements of standard 747s eventually meant that they could also operate economically on such routes. The basic 747-200 could carry a typical payload over distances of 6,000 miles or more and was also offered as a dedicated freighter with an upward hinging nose door (747-200F) or as a Combi passenger/cargo aircraft with a side-loading cargo door aft of the wing. Given the flexibility offered by such options, coupled with the aircraft's reliability and safety levels demonstrated in airline service, it is not surprising to record that Boeing succeeded in delivering no fewer than 643 examples of the 747 -100 and 200. Passenger reaction was enthusiastic, the wide-bodied fuselage giving a tremendous impression of space, getting away from the claustrophobic tube-like feeling associated with conventional narrow-bodied aircraft. Some airlines utilised the small upper passenger deck behind the flightdeck as a bar and lounge area, reminiscent of the facilities offered in the postwar Stratocruisers, but economics eventually did away with such luxuries and most operators used the space to pack in more revenue earning passengers. In fact the numbers of passengers embarking and disembarking from each 747 arrival caused tremendous problems at the world's airports which had to be substantially enlarged and upgraded to deal with such flights, especially as the trend towards wide-bodied high capacity airliners really got under way with the arrival of two more contenders from the rival McDonnell Douglas and Lockheed stables.

Design of the McDonnell Douglas DC-10 started in 1966 when Boeing announced its new wide-bodied 747 and American Airlines issued a specification for a smaller, twin-engined, wide body for use on domestic routes. The McDonnell Douglas team decided that a slightly larger three-engined design would better fit the bill and American Airlines subsequently placed an order for 25 of the new DC-10s, followed shortly afterwards by United who ordered a further 30. With these orders in the bag, McDonnell Douglas pressed ahead and by the end of 1970 had three development aircraft flying, while commercial services commenced in August 1971 on the busy American Airlines route from Chicago to Los Angeles. The basic DC-10-10 weighed in at 430,000lb, could carry between 270 and 380 passengers according to cabin configuration and was powered by three 39,300lb thrust General Electric CF6-6D or 6K turbofans giving a range with maximum payload of 3,300 miles. 122 DC-10-10s were built and delivered to six US airlines and two foreign airlines, among the latter being Laker Airlines who introduced the concept of low fares on the transatlantic routes. Developments included the DC-10-15 intended for operation from hot and high airports and the Pratt & Whitney JT9D-powered long range DC-10-20, although the latter only flew in prototype form. The true long range variant, and the one which sold in greatest numbers, was the DC-10-30 which appeared in 1972 and was powered by various versions of the General Electric CF6-50 giving over 50,000lb thrust which allowed a gross take-off weight of between 530,000 and 590,000lb. This translated to additional fuel, including an extra fuel tank in the after cargo compartment in the extended range DC-10-30ER, so that range with maximum payload rose to over 4,000 miles. The final civil variant was the DC-10-40, developed from the -20 prototype, and was sold to Northwest Airlines and Japan Airlines. The more popular DC-10-30 was also produced in Combi and Freighter versions and total civil sales of the DC-10 came to 386 aircraft although another 60 were completed

The sheer size of the Boeing 747 spawned a new name: the Jumbo Jet. Even today, the 747 is a monster among minnows, and this 1960s-vintage aircraft has proved the reliability and durability of its design time and time again since the first flight in 1969. In October 1993 the 1,000th 747 was delivered and it still serves in 15 variations with the majority of the world's biggest airlines. The sheer number of people disgorging from just one 747, let alone more, caused immense problems to the airports of the day and heralded the need for massive improvements to airport infrastructure and equipment.

Here, British Airways Boeing 747-136 G-AWNI is seen in Antigua. The British carrier BOAC saw the 747's potential and placed orders as early as 1966; these were taken over by BA on its formation in 1972 and, as well as 18 747-136s, of which G-AWNI was one, over 60 747s have flown with BA.

as military KC-10s. Production ended in 1989. The DC-10 was a fine aircraft and almost 300 remain in service today, examples of the long range Series 30 being particularly sought after. However during its career the DC-10 suffered a number of high profile fatal accidents and earned an undeserved reputation as an unsafe aircraft. These included the loss of a Turkish Airlines' aircraft in 1974 shortly after take-off from Paris in which 346 people were killed, another take-off accident in 1979 when an American Airlines aircraft crashed killing 279 passengers and crew, and the bizarre loss of an Air New Zealand DC-10-30 which flew into Mount Erebus in Antarctica, again with a large loss of life. While none of these were directly attributable to the basic design, public confidence waned and McDonnell Douglas went through a difficult period.

The other wide-bodied contemporary of the DC-10 was the Lockheed L1011 TriStar, which flew in late 1970 and was particularly significant in that, from the start, it was offered only with British-built Rolls-Royce RB211-524 turbofans in the 42,000 to 50,000lb thrust bracket and which offered particularly good fuel consumption characteristics. However development of both the airframe and engines led Lockheed and Rolls-Royce to the edge of bankruptcy and delayed the development and test programme by several months. The original short/medium range TriStar 1 had a maximum take-off weight of 430,000lb and could carry a maximum payload (between 256 and 400 passengers) over a range of 2,880 miles. It was bought by a number of airlines including Air Canada, Eastern, Delta and TWA, while in the UK it was sold to British Airways and Court Line. As with the DC-10, the TriStar saw considerable development, the first derivative being the TriStar 100 certificated at higher gross weight (450,000lb) to increase range. When fitted with uprated RB211s for operation from hot and high airfields, this became the TriStar 200. To compete with the DC-10-30, the long range TriStar 500 was developed, with a shorter fuselage seating between 246 and 300 passengers. Gross weight was increased to 496,000lb and 50,000lb thrust RB211-524B turbofans were fitted, this combination resulting in a range of 4,310 miles with maximum payload. The TriStar was an attractive aircraft with a good performance but orders were slow to materialise and Lockheed ended production after 250 aircraft, and in doing so ended its long association in the civil airliner market.

Although Lockheed had bowed out, Boeing and McDonnell Douglas did not have the market in wide-bodied aircraft to themselves as there was now a new and powerful name in the airliner manufacturing business – the European-based Airbus consortium. The roots of this organisation went back to the mid-1960s when various European manufacturers were look-

The McDonnell Douglas DC-10 never quite reached the sales levels anticipated of it, 386 being produced along with 60 of its military version – the KC-10 Extender, a long-range tanker/transporter – rather than the 1,000+ the company expected. This was due partly to a series of high-profile accidents – including two involving the rear cargo door, although the others were unrelated – partly because of competition from the Lockheed TriStar, partly because of the success of Airbus Industrie's advent into the market-place in the mid-1970s and probably most of all because of the slump of the 1980s. However, a stretched DC-10 derivative, the MD-11, first flew in 1990 and with over 150 sold or on order, combined DC-10/MD-11 family production has proved substantial.

Pictured is DC-10-30 D-ADQO of Condor Flugdienst in July 1989. Formed in 1961, Condor is a subsidiary of Lufthansa and bought DC-10-30s to replace 747s when charter market numbers declined.

ing at the possibility of producing a 200-300-seater for use on short and medium ranges routes within Europe. The costs of such a project were enough to make international collaboration necessary and one such group consisted of Hawker Siddeley, Breguet and Nord which produced a twin-engined design under the designation HBN-100, while Dassault and Sud Aviation came up with the very similar Galion and BAC offered the BAC 2-11 and 3-11. In 1967 a consortium was formed which comprised Aérospatiale from France, Hawker Siddeley from Britain and MBB from West Germany, as well as CASA from Spain and the Dutch Fokker company. Work commenced on the detailed design of what was to become the Airbus A300 based on work already carried out on the HBN-100 but although most of the companies concerned had various amounts of government backing, the British government pulled out in 1969 leaving Hawker Siddeley (later British Aerospace) to continue financing its original 12 percent share from its own resources (this was increased to 20 percent in 1978). In December 1970, Airbus Industrie was formed with headquarters at Toulouse in France to oversee the development, manufacture and marketing of the A300 although construction was spread around all the partners with Britain being responsible for the wing assemblies. After much debate, the General Electric CF6 turbofan was chosen as the powerplant, although Pratt & Whitney JT9D-59A engines were later offered as an option.

The first Airbus A300 eventually took-off from Toulouse, where Airbus final assembly was carried out, on 28 October 1972 and the production A300B2 flew in the following June. Compared to the original B1 model, this had a fuselage lengthened by 8ft 9in, gross weight was 302,000lb and it could carry 267 passengers in a typical mixed class layout or up to 375 in a high density configuration. In 1974 Airbus introduced the A300B4, which was certified at a higher gross weight to allow more fuel to be carried. This version had a range of 3,150 miles with 269 passengers. The A300 entered service in 1974 with Air France and proved to be reliable and economic in service. In fact it could match the DC-10 and TriStar in many aspect of payload/range performance using the fuel burnt by only two instead of three engines. Nevertheless, sales success was slow to come and only 53 firm orders had been placed by the end of 1977. This was partly due to airline reticence to order any new aircraft following the massive rise in fuel prices in the mid-1970s. A breakthrough came in 1978 when Eastern Airlines placed a large order following successful trials with four leased aircraft. Other orders began to roll in and by mid-1980 the total had risen to 194. Airbus continued development of the A300 with a convertible freighter version (A300C4) and also introduced the concept of the Forward Facing Crew Cockpit (FFCC) which relied on extensive automation to do away with the flight engineer, previously regarded as indispensable on large aircraft, so that the aircraft could be flown and operated by two or three pilots.

Like the DC-10, the Lockheed TriStar was affected by competition and recession, with the company lucky to survive the financial difficulties experienced by it and Rolls-Royce, whose RB211 engines powered the TriStar. Even the outstanding Series 500, a longer range development could not help significantly and production ceased in 1983 with one short of 250 produced.

This 500, Angola Airlines CS-TEC, is seen in June 1991.

With the A300 established, Airbus began to look at the market for a smaller stablemate: this evolved into the A310 which flew in April 1982. Employing the same fuselage cross-section as the A300, the A310 was approximately 20ft shorter and could seat between 218 and 280 passengers in eight abreast layout. The wing was entirely new and considerably more efficient than that of the A300, while power was provided by two 50,000lb thrust Pratt & Whitney JT9D-7R4E or General Electric CF6-80C2 turbofans. The A310 also introduced the concept of the 'glass' cockpit in which the multitude of conventional analogue instruments are replaced by a small number (normally four or six) computerised CRT displays. While this is normal practice today, Airbus was very much a pioneer in the introduction of such systems. In fact the new flightdeck was also applied to the new stretched A300-600 which appeared in 1983, followed by the definitive long range A300-600R in 1987. This version had a range of 4,340 miles with maximum payload and is currently the only version of the A300 still in production, total orders for all versions having reached 472 by the end of 1996. The smaller A310 had sold 261 examples in the same period and also remains in production. The success of Airbus certainly dented sales of American manufacturers and finally began to provide realistic and sustained competition for the first time since the end of World War 2.

For once, the Russian answer to new western designs did not appear to be a direct copy, although it was 1976 before their first wide-bodied airliner took to the air. This was the four-engined Ilyushin Il-86 which could carry up to 350 passengers in nine abreast seating. The chosen powerplant was 28,660lb thrust Kuznetsov NK-86 turbofan, but with a maximum take-off weight of 458,560lb, the aircraft was distinctly underpowered and its range with maximum payload was less than 2,000 miles. Aeroflot began scheduled services with the Il-86 in 1980, almost 10 years after the American wide bodies had entered service and total production was only around 100 aircraft, of which over 90 remain in service, some re-engined with more powerful and efficient Soloviev PS-90A turboprops.

The introduction during the 1970s of a new generation of wide-bodied airliners stimulated the air transport industry as air fares began to fall dramatically and millions of new passengers took to the skies. This effect was felt throughout the industry and stimulated the oper-

In a world dominated by massive American companies – Boeing, Douglas, Lockheed – it is remarkable just how successful the multi-national European Airbus project has proved. With over 450 sales, the A300 has served with many airlines, the breakthrough US customer being Eastern Airlines which took 30 – giving the Europeans a slice of the American market. The late lamented Pan Am leased A300s prior to purchasing A310s: this is N210PA in March 1988.

ations of smaller airlines at the other end of the scale. This was helped by the parallel development of a new breed of small turboprop commuter airliners seating between 19 and 50 passengers, and bringing new levels of comfort to short range feeder operations. One of the earliest examples was the de Havilland Canada DHC-6 Twin Otter which first flew in 1965 and subsequently sold 844 units up to 1988. Powered by two Pratt & Whitney PT6A turboprops, this simple and rugged little aircraft could carry 19 passengers at a speed of around 160kts and was widely used by third level airlines around the world. Although unpressurised, it brought turboprop-level performance and comfort to the remotest airstrips and also enabled small provincial centres to have direct links to major international airports. De Havilland Canada followed up this success with the much larger four-engined 44-54 seater Dash 7 which made a great virtue of its short take-off and landing (STOL) performance. This aircraft was pressurised and cruised at 220kts. The manufacturers hoped that a network of city STOL airports would be set up but, with a few prominent exceptions such as London's Docklands Airport which opened in 1987, this did not happen and only 111 Dash 7s were built.

In the UK, the twin-engined 30-seater Shorts 330 flew in 1974 and was also powered by the PT6A turboprop. Almost 200 were sold and the type was popular with American commuter airlines as its capacious square-section fuselage allowed comfortable three abreast seating and full standing headroom for passengers and cabin crew. The stretched Shorts 360, seating 36 passengers, flew in 1981 and was distinguishable by its single swept tailfin which replaced the twin fin and rudder arrangement of the earlier 330. Approximately 150 Shorts 330/360s remain in service today.

A surprise successful entrant in the small turboprop sweepstakes was the Brazilian company EMBRAER, whose EMB-110 Bandeirante was developed from a military transport. The definitive EMB-110P2 flew in 1977, subsequently becoming a best seller with over 500 examples (including military versions) produced. Powered by two of the ubiquitous PT6A turboprops, the Bandeirante could seat up to 21 passengers, although it was normally configured as a 19-seater. It was unpressurised but its clean low wing design with a retractable undercarriage endowed it with a cruising speed of around 185kts.

Demand for pressurised small turboprop airliners that could climb above the weather resulted in British Aerospace reviving the Jetstream, which originally flew as far back as 1967. The revised 19-seater Jetstream 31 powered by two 940shp Garrett TPE331 turboprops flew in 1980 and proved very successful. Over 300 were sold, many to American regional and commuter airlines. However, once again EMBRAER achieved a major success, this time with the EMB-120 Brasilia which flew in 1983 powered by two 1,800shp Pratt & Whitney Canada PW118 turboprops. Seating up to 30 passengers, the Brasilia cruised at 260kts at an altitude of 25,000ft – almost jetlike performance which attracted orders for over 500 aircraft.

While small turboprops were coming into widespread use, their larger counterparts such as the Fokker Friendship and Hawker Siddeley 748 were facing competition from a new breed of small jet airliners. First to appear was the Fokker F28 Fellowship which flew in 1967 and began commercial operations with LTU in 1969. The F28 was produced to complement the F27 turboprop and the original Mk 1000 was a 65-seater powered by two 9,850lb thrust Rolls-Royce RB183 Spey Juniors. The F28 Mk 2000 was a stretched version seating up to 79 passengers. It appeared in 1971 while the Mks 5000 and 6000 were similar but with increased wingspan and more powerful engines. These improvements were applied retrospectively to the earlier models which were then designated Mk 3000 and Mk 4000 respectively. The latter became the major production version; a gross weight rise to 71,000lb and a redesigned interior allowed up to 85 passengers to be carried. Although produced by Fokker, the F28 had a considerable British content including the wings, engines and undercarriage. A total of 241 was produced up to 1986. Fokker was also involved in the production of another rather unusual small jet airliner, the German VFW614 which made its first flight from Bremen in July 1971. Seating between 34 and 44 passengers, this was the smallest jet airliner to enter production up to that time and it was powered by two 7,760lb thrust Rolls-Royce M45H turbofans mounted in pylons above the wing, a unique configuration which has not been repeated on any other airliner design. Only a handful were produced for Cimber Air (Denmark), TAT and Air Alsace. The VFW614 was an interesting attempt to produce a small regional jet airliner but its operating economics were unattractive compared to contemporary turboprops and it was, perhaps, a little ahead of its time.

1980s to Date

In the 1970s the success of Airbus in developing the wide-bodied A300 spurred Boeing into accelerating its plans for two new generation airliners which eventually emerged as the Boeing 757 and 767. While designing these aircraft, Boeing made a conscious effort to retain as much commonality between the two aircraft despite their difference in size: one result was that both had an identical flightdeck including the latest EFIS displays and integrated flight management systems. The smaller of the two was the Boeing 757 which retained a six abreast seating with a single central aisle and was intended as a replacement for the best selling Boeing 727 tri-jet with the emphasis on greatly reducing fuel costs. The new aircraft was to be powered by two 40,100lb thrust Rolls-Royce RB211-535 turbofans, making it the first Boeing design to be launched with British engines, although alternative Pratt & Whitney PW2037 engines were later offered as an option. With a take-off weight of over 220,000lb, the 757 was considerably larger than the 727 which it was intended to replace. However, by Boeing standards the new aircraft was a slow seller with only 240 ordered six years after its first flight. This was partly due to the longevity of the 727 which just kept going as the workhorse of many major airlines who saw little point in investing in new technology. This situation was soon to change when the ETOPS concept was introduced in the late 1980s, the acronym standing for Extended Range Twin Operations which permitted the use of suitable twin-engined airliners on long over water routes. Prior to this the international rules governing such flights had, with some exceptions, required twin-engined aircraft to be flown on routes so that they were never more than 60 minutes flying time at single engine speed from a suitable airfield. This was intended to cover the case of an unscheduled shutdown of one of the engines but the reliability of the modern turbofans was such that complete shutdowns were statistically very rare. After considerable debate involving aircraft and engine manufacturers, airlines and regulatory authorities, it was accepted that the 60-minute requirement could be doubled to 120 minutes and, when further experience was gained, some aircraft and airlines were permitted to extend this to 180 minutes.

The effect of this procedure was dramatic and aircraft such as the Boeing 757 and 767, and the Airbus A300/310, were the immediate beneficiaries, most being offered in new ER (Extended Range) configuration to take advantage of the new regulations. The 757 began to appear on many transoceanic long haul routes, being particularly popular with European charter operators and also with airlines flying scheduled services on such routes where demand was not enough to fill large aircraft such as the DC-10 or Boeing 747. Orders for the 757 began to build up and currently over 850 have been ordered, including 75 of the Boeing 757-200PF, a cargo version aimed at the US small parcels freight market. Unusually for a modern airliner, the 757 has been virtually unmodified for its 15-year production life up to 1996 when Boeing finally decided to offer a stretched version, the 757-300. This will have a 23ft fuselage stretch, increasing passenger capacity to around 240 and will appeal to charter airlines such as Condor Flugdienst, the launch customer.

Chronologically, the 757 was preceded by its big brother, the wide-bodied Boeing 767 which first flew in September 1981 powered by two 48,000lb thrust Pratt & Whitney JT9D-7R4 turbofans, although later versions offered the more powerful PW4050 series or General Electric CF6-80C2 engines. The big 767 could seat up to 290 passengers if an eight abreast seating configuration was adopted but a more typical load was around 220 in a mixed class layout with seven abreast seating in the main cabin. Initial deliveries were made to United Airlines, which had ordered 30 of the original 767-200s, but the 767-200ER made its appearance in 1984 and it was with one of these aircraft that El Al started the world's first ETOPS commercial flights with non-stop services from Tel Aviv to Canada and the United States. Externally the -200ER was identical to the -200, the main difference being an increase in maximum weight from 300,000lb to 345,000lb to allow extra fuel to be carried. A stretched 767-300 appeared in 1986 with the ER version flying later the same year, apart from a longer fuselage accommodating up to 45 extra passengers, the -300 also offered customer airlines the choice of powerplants from all three major manufacturers (Pratt & Whitney, General Electric and Rolls-Royce). The -300ER was first put into commercial service by American Airlines in February 1988 while a dedicated 767-300F freighter was delivered to UPS in October 1995, the first of 32 on order. Over 700 Boeing 767s have been ordered, the larger -300 outselling the smaller -200 by a margin of two to one and a further stretched version, dubbed the 767-400X, is currently under active consideration by Boeing.

While Boeing was investing in the development of two completely new aircraft, it did not neglect the older 747 Jumbo which was the cornerstone of its fortunes and whose continued sales success helped to finance its smaller brethren. In October 1983 the first of a new model, the 747-300, took to the air. This was basically a -200 series with the upper deck behind the flightdeck extended to accommodate up to 91 passengers, thus boosting the theoretical maximum seating capacity to 630, although a more typical mixed class layout carried around 426. As a simple derivative version, the -300 was quickly certificated and entered service

One of the most successful medium-range airliners of recent years, the Boeing 757 benefited from ETOPS which allowed it to be used on transoceanic operations. Pictured here in November 1990, Boeing 757-236ER – ER for extended range – G-BPEC was called Loch Katrine *when under Caledonian Airlines, the charter arm of the British Airways fleet. Caledonian was sold in December 1994 and G-BPEC has returned to BA service.*

Another massive success for Boeing, the 767 is in service with over 70 airlines including United Airlines which has over 30. Here N656UA, one of United's 767-322ERs, is seen landing at Heathrow in September 1993. The 767-300 is the stretched version of the aircraft which entered service in November 1986. The 767-300ER carries up to 290 passengers to a max range of nearly 7,000 miles.

with Swissair in March 1983. Maximum weight rose to 833,000lb and the range with a full payload was now 6,500 miles. Despite these excellent figures, the 747-300 sold in relatively small numbers with only 81 ordered. However this was not because of any problems with this version but simply because Boeing subsequently offered the airlines a substantially redesigned new version, the 747-400 which first flew in April 1988 and entered service, initially with Northwest Airlines, early the following year. This turned out to be the most popular version of the 747 and currently over well over 500 are on order and almost 400 are actually in service. Boeing has had to raise production to four aircraft a month in order to keep up with demand.

Although retaining the same fuselage dimensions as the -300, the new -400 was almost a new aircraft in virtually every other respect. The flightdeck was completely redesigned for a two-pilot crew using the latest EFIS technology and an advanced flight management system. There were several aerodynamic improvements, the most noticeable being an increased wingspan with upturned winglets, and composite materials were used in several areas to achieve a reduction in empty weight. Finally, uprated engines in the 52-58,000lb thrust rating were offered from all three major manufacturers. The sum of all these changes resulted in an aircraft capable of carrying the same payload as the -300 over ranges up to 7,300 miles at a seat/mile cost reduced by up to 13 percent. As further evidence of the flexibility of the design, it is offered in Combi and Freighter versions while the 747-400D is a special variant for the Japanese domestic market. So successful is the 747-400 that it has now supplanted all other versions in production, the last of the so-called 'classic' 747s being delivered in 1991. On 10 September 1993 Boeing passed a notable milestone when it rolled out the 1,000th Boeing 747, only the fourth jet airliner to have reached that total, all the others also being Boeing products (707, 727, 737).

In contrast to America and western Europe, Russia has had little success with its attempts to produce a wide-bodied airliner, the Il-86 having suffered from major performance deficiencies. In an effort to improve matters, and in a timescale almost identical to the Boeing 747-400 programme, Ilyushin completely redesigned the four-engined Il-86 to produce the slightly smaller but much more efficient Il-96 which flew in September 1988. Although the fuselage was shorter, seating a maximum of 300 passengers, and empty weight was reduced, the redesigned long span wings with prominent winglets coupled with more powerful 35,000lb thrust Soloviev PS-90A turbofans, resulted in a much better performance.

Maximum payload could now be carried over ranges of almost 6,000 miles – not quite up to figures achieved by its Airbus and Boeing counterparts, but respectable nonetheless. As with the 747-400, the Ilyushin design featured a new electronic flightdeck but went one step further with an advanced fly-by-wire flight control system. While the Il-96 is undoubtedly a capable aircraft, it was produced at a time when the break-up of the Soviet Union meant that the structure of civil aviation in the new Confederation of Independent States (CIS) changed completely. Many of the new eastern bloc airlines were able to opt for the purchase or lease of western aircraft. Consequently only 12 of the basic Il-96-300s have been ordered, although in 1992 the first westernised Il-96M was produced in association with the American company Rockwell Collins. With a fuselage stretched to carry up to 375 passengers, the Il-96M is powered by Pratt & Whitney PW2037 engines and is fitted with improved avionics including some American components. Prospects for this version look much better and 25 are on order, including 20 for ARIA (Aeroflot Russian International Airlines).

The Ilyushin design which has probably made the most impact in the west is the Il-76 freighter. This four-engined high-wing design originally flew in 1971 as a military freighter but civil versions were produced for Aeroflot. With the opening up of east/west relationships in the early 1990s, the sturdy Russian freighter found itself much in demand by specialist cargo operators as there was no direct western equivalent. The most powerful version is the Il-76MF which has four Perm PS-90AN turbofans and can carry a maximum 115,000lb payload over a range of almost 2,000 miles with loading and unloading being facilitated by the military style rear loading ramp. Over 850 civil and military versions have been built and the type remains in production today.

Although Ilyushin builds large aircraft, when it comes to size the company is completely outclassed by the Ukraine-based Antonov which over the years has specialised in large freight aircraft. For many years the An-10 and An-12 four-engined turboprops, which dated back to 1957, were common sights around the world and were produced in both freight and passenger versions. In the 1960s Antonov produced the massive An-22 freighter, powered by four 15,000shp Kuznetsov turboprops and intended as a military freighter. Projected civil versions, never built, would have carried over 700 passengers! More recently, in 1982, Antonov flew the An-124 Ruslan freighter, which is capable of carrying a 150-tonne load over a distance of 2,800 miles. Powered by four ZMKB Progress D-18T turbofans, the Ruslan was also conceived as a military freighter but has found widespread application for civil purposes and there are plans to produce a westernised version with General Electric CF6-80 turbofans and Western avionics and navigation systems. It is believed that around 50 Ruslans have been produced to date. Not content with these giants, Antonov also went on to produce what is currently the world's largest aircraft, the six-engined An-225 Mriya (Dream). With an all-up weight of over 1,300,000lb, the An-225 can carry a 250-tonne payload although the power of its 53,800lb thrust Lotarev D-18T turbofans are enough to lift it off relatively short 1,000m runways.

Another Russian jet airliner which has been married to western technology is the twin-engined Tupolev Tu-204 which, at first glance, is almost indistinguishable from the Boeing 757 apart from prominent winglets. This was designed as successor to the Tu-154 and first flew in 1989. It featured a fully automated flightdeck with advanced avionics and a triplicated digital fly-by-wire control system. Of similar size and capacity to the Boeing 757, the Russian aircraft can carry up to 214 passengers and is powered by 35,275lb thrust Perm PS90A turbofans; a higher gross weight version is designated Tu-214. A westernised version powered by Rolls-Royce RB211-535E4B turbofans is marketed as the Tu-224 and production of all three versions is actually carried out by a company called Aviastar. A further development is the Tu-234, launched in September 1995. This is a short fuselage lightweight version of the basic design carrying up to 160 passengers although, at the time of writing, it has not flown. Problems obtaining the necessary funding have held back the development of other

Tupolev projects, including the Tu-304 long-range wide-bodied twin powered by Rolls-Royce Trent 884 turbofans, the Tu-330 freighter derived from the Tu-204 and the 100-seater Tu-334 which is currently flying in prototype form.

A feature of many modern jet airliners has been their longevity, many remaining in service with their original owners for more than 20 years. This has meant that several basically sound designs have been overtaken by developments in engines, avionics and construction methods but the cost of developing a completely new aircraft to incorporate such advances has not made commercial sense. Consequently the appearance of completely new airliners is becoming comparatively rare with the major manufacturers preferring to improve their existing and established products. This process is best illustrated by the career of two of the world's best selling airliners, the DC-9 and the Boeing 737. As already related, the DC-9 had proved itself extremely adaptable and was produced in a number of major sub-variants. In 1977 a major new development was announced. This was initially known as the DC-9 Super 80 and it made its first flight in October 1979. Compared to earlier models, the Super 80 had an even longer fuselage, now almost 148ft long, and carrying up to 172 passengers — more than twice the capacity of the original DC-9-10. To maintain performance Pratt & Whitney JT9D 200 series engines giving 18,000lb of thrust were fitted and maximum take-off weight rose to 140,000lb. The cabin interior was modernised to give a more spacious appearance and the aircraft's systems and avionics were updated. The first of 15 Super 80s were delivered to Swissair, the launch customer, in 1980 and a number of further developments known as the DC-9 Super 81/82 and 83 were also planned.

At the beginning of the 1980s McDonnell Douglas decided to give the DC-9 a completely new image, while at the same time raising the company's image amongst the travelling public at the same time as distancing itself from the Douglas name which it had inherited when the original companies merged in 1967. Consequently the Super 80 and its derivatives became known as the McDonnell Douglas MD-80 series and the basic model described above became the MD-81. When fitted with uprated 20,000lb thrust JT8D-217A turbofans for improved airfield performance the designation became MD-82, and this version had a maximum take-off weight raised to 149,500lb. This appeared in 1981 and was followed in 1984 by the MD-83 with even more powerful engines, a take-off weight of 160,000lb and greater fuel capacity. All three of these had the long fuselage but the MD-87, ordered by Finnair and Austrian airlines, was basically an MD-82 with a shorter fuselage seating 114-139 passengers but with improved airfield performance and greater range (up to 2,833 miles with full payload). This made its first flight in December 1986 and in 1987 was fol-

There are remarkable visual similarities between the Tupolev Tu-204 and the Boeing 757 – as there are between so many western and Russian aircraft. It's a modern aircraft which makes use of composite materials, fly-by-wire, an EFIS cockpit and winglets. Capable of carrying more than 200 passengers over 2,000 miles, it is offered with a variety of engines – Russian (Soloviev PS-90A turbofans), British (RB211-535 turbofans) or US (Pratt & Whitney PW2240s).

This is CCCP-64006 at Farnborough in September 1992. BRAVIA is the now defunct British Russian Aviation Corporation which funded the RB211-535-engined version. Late in 1996 the programme received a boost when the Egyptian Kato Group ordered 30 aircraft which it hoped to lease to mainly Russian and CIS airlines.

lowed by the final MD-80 variant, the MD-88 which was identical to the MD-82 except for the incorporation of an advanced electronic flightdeck and improved cabin interior. This entered service with Delta Airlines in 1988.

The MD-80 series proved even more popular than the early DC-9 models from which it was derived and a total of 1,160 has been ordered; virtually all of these have now been delivered. However this was by no means the end of the story and in 1989 the company formally announced the next stage in the development of this remarkable airframe. This was the MD-90, which has a fuselage stretched by another 6ft and is powered by two 28,000lb thrust IAE V2500 turbofans, giving a range of around 2,400 miles with a reduced fuel burn. It also has a new Electronic Flight Information System (EFIS) flightdeck, carbonfibre brakes and a modernised cabin interior. The main production version is expected to be the MD-90-30 while a projected MD-90-50 will be able to fly up to 3,450 miles with a load of 153 passengers. A total of 143 MD-90s had been ordered by the end of 1996.

The final DC-9 derivative is the MD-95, which was launched in October 1995 with an order for 50 aircraft from the low cost US airline Valuejet. Powered by two BMW/Rolls-Royce BR715 turbofans, the MD-95 is expected to fly early in 1998 with deliveries from June 1999. However the future of this product is in some doubt and it is possible that production may be transferred to China, already producing the MD-80 under licence from McDonnell Douglas.

The other long-lived design, and currently the world's best selling airliner, is the Boeing 737. By the beginning of the 1980s this incredibly successful aircraft was beginning to look a bit long in the tooth. Boeing therefore initiated a major upgrade which resulted in three new versions. All of these were powered by new CFM56 turbofans which, because of their increased diameter, required a complete redesign of the engine mountings, and all had a revised flightdeck incorporating EFIS technology and automated engine controls. The wing was slightly increased in span and some detailed aerodynamic improvements were incorporated. The first of the new breed was the 737-300 which had a 10ft fuselage stretch, increasing capacity to 150 passengers; this flew in 1984 to be followed in February 1988 by the even longer 737-400 which could carry up to 169 passengers. The last of the trio was the 108-seater 737-500 which flew in 1989 and retained the short fuselage of the earlier 737-200 but incorporated all the other refinements of the new generation 737s. Together these three 737 variants have been incredibly successful with 1,922 having been ordered by the end of 1996, making a total of 3,066 since the original 737 flew back in 1967.

But even this is not the end of the story as Boeing recently launched the third generation of the 737 family, again a trio of models designated the 600, 700 and 800 respectively. The first two replace the short fuselage 737-500 and the longer 737-300 respectively while the -800, which will replace the -400, is just over 9ft longer and will be able to carry up to 189 passengers. All the new models will have a completely redesigned wing with span increased by just over 16ft to give a 25 percent increase in wing area and a 30 percent increase in fuel capacity. Power will be provided by CFM56-7 engines rated at between 18,500 and 26,400lb thrust depending on the application and model. The first of the new 737s will fly early in 1997, but already the order book stands at 426 and to meet this demand Boeing is planning to raise production to 17 aircraft a month by the end of 1997. First deliveries of the new 737-700 should be to Southwest Airlines in October 1997, while Hapag Lloyd should get the first 737-800 in April 1998 and SAS will take delivery of the first 737-600 in August 1998. Already the 737 has been in production for over 30 years and, given the interest shown in the latest versions, it will undoubtedly be produced for many years to come.

In contrast to the derivative nature of the MD-80/90 and the various 737 developments, Airbus had to start with a clean sheet when it decided to produce a medium-sized narrow-bodied twin-jet. Launched in 1984, it subsequently made its maiden flight on 22 April 1987. In the same class as the Boeing 737, and of similar configuration, the Airbus A320 was well received by passengers; the most significant feature of the aircraft is the flightdeck with its distinctive sidesticks instead of conventional control columns pointing to the fact that this aircraft employs a computer-driven fly-by-wire control system. When the pilot applies pressure to the sidestick (which actually moves only very slightly) the flight control system computers ensure that the control response is such that the aircraft will always remain in a safe operating envelope. Thus, for example, if the pilot was to attempt to overbank in a turn at low speed, a conventional aircraft would stall and possibly enter a spin whereas the A320 would automatically limit the angle of bank and, if necessary, automatically increase the engine thrust to maintain a safe flying attitude. All flight instrumentation, navigation information and systems status is shown is shown on six interchangeable electronic display screens and the aircraft's sophisticated flight management system takes care of almost all the routine tasks associated with a flight. The A320 is powered by two 25,000lb thrust IAE V2500 or CFM56-5-A1 turbofans and with a maximum payload of 150 passengers has a range of 2,930 miles. First deliveries were made to Air France in March 1988 and since then the A320 has recorded no less than 787 orders up to August 1996.

With the basic aircraft established, Airbus launched a stretched version, the A321 seating up to 185 passengers, in November 1989. This has more powerful (30,000lb thrust) versions of the V2500 and CFM56 engines and entered service with Lufthansa in 1994 while other customers include Alitalia, Austrian Airlines, Gulf Air and Iberia, bringing total orders to 177 (up to August 1996). An uprated A321-200 is scheduled to enter service at the end of 1996: this has increased weights and fuel capacity for use in the Inclusive Tour charter market. The other A320 derivative is the short fuselage A319 which seats 124 passengers and was launched in June 1993 with first deliveries being made, in May 1996, to Swissair. Other large orders have been received from Air Canada and Lufthansa. At the end of 1996, total orders for all three models (A319, 320 and 321) had reached 1,110 of which 613 had actually been delivered. Considering that the aircraft has been in service for less than a decade, this is a remarkable achievement and Airbus claims that this is the fastest selling airliner family currently in production.

While Boeing, McDonnell Douglas and Airbus carved up the market for large and medium-sized jet airliners, other manufacturers attempted to fill perceived gaps at the lower end of the jet spectrum. One of these was British Aerospace which had been formed in 1977 by the merger of the British Aircraft Corporation and the Hawker Siddeley Group, themselves the product of previous multiple mergers in the 1960s. BAe was keen to launch an airliner product in order to establish its name and chose the Hawker Siddeley HS146 design for a four-engined high-wing aircraft carrying between 70 and 100 passengers. Progress on this had been slow during the 1970s while the future shape of the British aircraft industry was under review by the government, but with the setting up of the nationalised British Aerospace a go ahead was given to the prototype, now known as the BAe146, which eventually flew for the first time on 3 September 1981. The powerplants were four 6,970lb thrust Textron Lycoming ALF502R turbofans carried on pylon mountings under the slightly swept wing. In this guise the 146-100 could carry up to 82 passengers in six abreast seating, or 70 in the more comfortable five abreast configuration favoured by most US airlines customers.

The 146 entered service with British independent airline Dan Air in 1983 while deliveries of the stretched 146-200 to Air Wisconsin began in 1983, this version seating 96-112 passengers. The 146 was something of a milestone in British aviation history as it was the first British airliner not powered by British engines and, in a reflection of the increasingly international nature of modern aircraft projects, the wings were built in America and the tail unit in Sweden. The 146 was not designed to compete head on with the established Boeing 737 and McDonnell Douglas DC-9/MD-80 but had other attributes intended to appeal to many airlines operating regional services. The relatively low-powered ALF502 turbofans were exceptionally quiet and this, coupled with the aircraft's good airfield performance and four-

engined safety levels, allowed the aircraft to operate from many airfields which were closed to its competitors on safety or environmental grounds. The final version of the 146 was the Series 300 which had an even longer fuselage allowing 112 passengers to be carried in five abreast comfort. Some 219 BAe146s were ordered and delivered before production ceased in favour of a new and much improved version in 1991.

Under a British Aerospace reorganisation, the 146 became the responsibility of a new division which took its name from one of Britain's famous aircraft manufacturers, Avro, and the aircraft was now known as the Avro RJ70, RJ85, RJ100 and RJ115. The letters RJ stood for Regional Jet and the first three effectively replaced the original 100, 200 and 300 Series models while the RJ115 was a high density version of the RJ100. The new Avro RJs all featured new uprated Allied Signal LF507 engines, higher gross weights, increased fuel capacity and digital avionics and flight management systems to permit Category III ILS operations. As with the original 146, all the RJs are also available as freighter, convertible or combi versions with an upward opening freight door on the portside rear fuselage. The RJ family has been aggressively marketed and over 100 have been ordered to date which makes the 146/Avro RJ the best selling British jet airliner.

A factor which may well prove to benefit the future sales prospects of the Avro RJ family was the unfortunate collapse of the Fokker company in 1996. This famous Dutch concern had developed its earlier F28 Fellowship into the Fokker 100 which first flew in 1986 and had proved to be a tough competitor for the BAe146. The Fokker 100 retained the overall configuration of its predecessor and was powered by two Rolls-Royce Tay 620 turbofans each delivering 13,850lb of thrust. It could seat up to 107 passengers in a lengthened fuselage and a considerable number of detailed improvements had been made, including the provision of the now mandatory electronic flightdeck and full Category III operating capability. The first customer was Swissair but orders were received from around the world and the Fokker 100 did particularly well in South America and the Far East, as well as picking up major orders from US Air and American Airlines. In 1995 the short fuselage Fokker 70 entered service, this derivative being aimed at the rising demand for small regional jets which were beginning to replace some of the larger turboprops. Approximately 30 of these had been sold when Fokker ended production in early 1997 and a famous name sadly departed from the aviation scene.

While Fokker and British Aerospace competed in the market for 70-100-seater short range jets, a new breed of small regional airliner was also beginning to challenge the

Swissair was the first operator of the Airbus A319. It seats 124 passengers and is the smallest member of the Airbus family with a shortened (111ft) fuselage. A derivative of the A320, the A319 has the longest range of the A320 family, at just over 3,000 miles. Immensely successful, this series of aircraft has seen over 500 sales with many more on order. Air Canada was the first North American airline to take the A319, the first of 35 aircraft being handed over in December 1996.

Originally designed by Hawker Siddeley, the BAe146 was developed as a short-range, short take-off airliner. Renowned for its quietness, it has been allowed into city airports – like London City – where proximity to urban areas usually precludes jet aircraft. Powered by four Textron Lycoming turbofans, over 200 were built before the designation changed again as part of a British Aerospace reorganisation. Over 300 RJ70/85/100 and 115s have been built – making it the most successful of all British-built airliners. The 299th and 300th aircraft were called Lombardia *and* Piedmonte *and went to Azurra Air on 5 December 1996. This is BAe146 G-OLCA in the colours of Jersey European.*

supremacy of the turboprops in the form of the Canadair (now Bombardier) Regional Jet which was a 50-seater based on the successful Challenger business jet. The Canadair RJ flew in 1991 and over 100 are now in service with airlines as diverse as Lufthansa Cityline, Lauda Air and Brittany Air in Europe, and Air Canada, Comair and Skywest in the United States. Not content with this, Bombardier has produced an Extended Range version and is working on the 70-seater CRJ-X which should fly in 1999. Powered by two General Electric CF34 turbofans, this will carry a maximum payload over a range of 1,700 miles. The RJ and CRJ-X do not, however, have this sector of the market to themselves. The Brazilian EMBRAER company has flown the very similar EMB-145 which is attracting much favourable comment from the airlines and looks set to equal the success of the turboprop Brasilia. Early design studies for the EMB-145 were based on a simple development of the Brasilia, retaining the straight wing but replacing the turboprops with Allison GMA-3007 turbofans. However the prototype, which flew on 11 August 1995, was quite different, with a swept wing and power improved by two tail-mounted Allison AE3007A turbofans. EMBRAER already holds firm orders for over 65 aircraft including a substantial commitment for 25 aircraft plus up to 175 options from Continental Express.

These new regional jets will eventually supplant the current stable of turboprop airliners which entered service during the 1980s. Several of these were derivatives of earlier designs including the Fokker 50 which followed on from the highly successful F27 Friendship. With

more powerful PW125B turboprops replacing the long-lived Rolls-Royce Darts, and a longer fuselage seating up to 58 passengers, the Fokker 50 could cruise at 245kts at altitudes up to 25,000ft. Modern avionics were fitted and the cabin interior considerably upgraded while Fokker paid particular attention to eliminating the vibration inherent in propeller-driven aircraft and claimed that the result gave a ride indistinguishable from that of jet in terms of smoothness and noise levels. Over 170 Fokker 50s are in service but production has ended following the collapse of the company in 1996. A potential rival was also a derivative design, the British Aerospace ATP (Advanced Turboprop) which was developed from the Hawker Siddeley 748 and was powered by two modern 2,330shp PW124 or 126 turboprops. This flew in 1982 and was slightly larger than the Fokker 50, seating up 68 passengers. Although in service with British Airways and British Midland, sales were slow as production ended after fewer than 60 aircraft were completed. British Aerospace is hoping for better luck with the smaller Jetstream 41 which is a 29-seat derivative of the 19-seater Jetstream 31. This is more than a simple stretch as the airframe has been substantially redesigned and power is provided by two 1,500shp Garrett TPE331-14GR turboprops giving an economical cruising speed of 260kts, very respectable for this class of aircraft.

Much more successful was the de Havilland Canada Dash 8, a sleek twin-engined high-winged 36-seater which was launched in 1983 and entered service the following year. Initial production model was the Dash 8 Series 100 and this was complemented by the 50-seater Series 300 which appeared in 1987. Building on the experience gained with earlier designs, the Dash 8 offers a sparkling high speed cruise performance while still retaining some of the STOL characteristics of the older four-engined Dash 7. This combination has resulted in a substantial order book with almost 400 Dash 8s in service around the world at the end of 1996. De Havilland (now owned by Bombardier) is working on the Dash 8 Series 400, launched at the 1995 Paris Airshow, which will offer a substantial increase in size and performance. A considerably longer fuselage will seat up to 70 passengers and more powerful turboprops will raise maximum cruising speed from 285 to 350kts. This will bring the Dash 8 into close competition with established regional jets such as the Avro RJ70 and is typical of a trend amongst the manufacturers of turboprops to raise performance levels. A typical example is the Swedish company Saab which produced the twin turboprop 35-seater Saab 340 in 1983. This cruised at around 260kts but has now been complemented by the 50-seater Saab 2000 which is capable of 360kts. Another fast performer is the Dornier Do328 which flew in 1991 and has sold moderately well to European and American airlines. This also cruises at well in excess of 300kts.

One of the most successful families of turboprops has come from an entirely new source – Avions de Transport Regional, otherwise known as ATR. This is a joint international company set up in 1981 by Aeritalia of Italy and Aérospatiale of France to design and build a new twin-engined turboprop regional airliner. The collaborative programme arose after each of the participating companies had initiated projects for similar aircraft in the late 1970s. Whereas many rival projects of the period were based on older designs, ATR was able to start with a clean sheet and produced an aircraft in which simplicity and economy of operation were the keynotes. The resultant ATR42 flew from Toulouse in August 1984, powered by two Pratt & Whitney PW120 turboprops; by that date ATR held orders for over 60 aircraft. Launch customers included Air Littoral and, in the United States, Command Air. The ATR42 was a high-wing 46-seater with the main undercarriage retracting into fairings on either side of the fuselage. Its Pratt & Whitney engines offered substantial fuel savings when compared to older similarly sized aircraft such as the HS748 and the Fokker Friendship and it soon proved to be reliable and easy to operate in everyday airline service. As well as improved versions of the ATR42 with uprated engines, the longer fuselage ATR72 was launched in 1985, subsequently making its first flight in October 1988. With two 2,400shp Pratt & Whitney PW124Bs, this could carry up to 74 passengers and was attractive to sev-

Avions de Transport Régional is the name given to the collaborative venture between what was then Aeritalia and Aérospatiale. The ATR42/72/82 family has picked up over 400 orders from a wide range of airlines since first flight in 1982 – as evinced by ATR42-312 NI8814 of Continental Express seen at Denver in June 1989. Powered by two P&W Canada turboprops (1,800shp ATR42 and 2,300shp for the ATR72), the ATR42 can carry 50 passengers over 3,000 miles; the ATR72 takes 74. The ATR82 has a further stretch to allow 82 passengers in total.

eral airlines which already operated the smaller ATR42. Such is the popularity of these aircraft that almost 450 ATR42s and 72s were in service by the end of 1996.

Few airlines operate a single type of aircraft but require a mix of capabilities to accommodate the demands of different routes and passenger levels. All manufacturers attempt to provide a range of models, hoping that they can persuade an airline to buy all their aircraft from a single source. On a large scale the most successful company in this respect is Boeing, which can offer aircraft from the smaller 737 to the largest 747. While this suits major airlines, such as British Airways, it does not help the smaller regional airlines whose requirements may range from small 19-seater commuter airliners up to 100-seater jets. In an effort to provide a complete range of aircraft, ATR recently joined forces with British Aerospace to set up a new marketing company known as Air International (Regional) which reduces to the convenient acronym AI(R). This can offer a complete spectrum of regional airlines starting with the Jetstream 31 and 41, through the ATR42 and 72, to the Avro RJ family. In the long term AI(R) is planning a brand new twin-jet known as the AIR70 which was launched in June 1996 and should fly in mid-2000 – possibly the first new airliner of the new millennium! This will be a 70-seater but a smaller 58-seater, not surprisingly designated AIR58, is also under consideration.

While ATR and AI(R) were creating a new success story for European manufacturers, the now well established Airbus was not standing still. When Boeing launched its 757 and 767 designs in the late 1970s, it was seen as direct challenge to the success of the Airbus consortium with its A300 and A310. In order to maintain its position, Airbus also went ahead with a pair of complementary designs which became the wide-bodied A330 and A340. In some respects these were actually the same aircraft as they had identical fuselages and similar wing structures, the most obvious difference being the powerplants. Whereas the A330 was a twin-jet, intended for high capacity medium to long range routes, the A340 was a four-engined aircraft with emphasis on ultra long range. The joint programme was initially launched in June 1987 after several years of projects and studies which investigated a wide range of wide and narrow body configurations before deciding on the wide-bodied twin-aisle configuration with eight abreast seating in the economy cabin and six abreast in First and Business. First to fly was the A340 which took to the air in October 1991. It was subsequently produced in two versions: the shorter A340-200 seating around 263 passengers in a three-class layout and the A340-300 with a lengthened fuselage carrying 295 passengers in a similar configuration. These entered service with Lufthansa and Air Inter respectively early in 1993. Optimised for very long range flights and powered by four 31,200lb thrust CFM56-5C-2 turbofans, the -200 can carry its payload over a range of 7,200 miles while the larger -300 can reach out to 7,300 miles. Currently under development is the A340-800 which, as its designation implies, will have the prodigious range of 8,000 miles!

The twin-engined A330 flew almost a year behind the A340, in November 1992, and the initial production variant was the long fuselage A330-300 which typically seated 335 passengers in two classes or 295 in a three class layout. This prototype was powered by two General Electric CF6-80C2 turbofans but production aircraft were offered with Pratt & Whitney PW4000s or Rolls-Royce RB211 Trents, the first time that the British manufacturer had succeeded in hanging one of its engines on an Airbus wing. All three engines offered ratings in the 64,000-72,000lb thrust bracket. At the time of its maiden flight, the A330 was the largest twin-jet airliner to have flown, and the A330/340 family is the largest ever to enter production in western Europe. The A330 entered service with Air Inter and Cathay Pacific early in 1994 and since then has gained orders for approximately 160 aircraft while the A340 has slightly more. Both aircraft have advanced flightdecks and automated control systems which have become the hallmark of Airbus aircraft and the manufacturers claim that they have around 60 percent more hold space than the Boeing 747, enabling operators to boost revenue by carrying substantial amounts of cargo on scheduled passenger services.

The demand for ultra long range aircraft has been partly fuelled by the booming economies of the Far East and Pacific rim countries, which has boosted demand for aircraft able to fly non-stop on routes such as London to Hong Kong, Tokyo and Singapore, or from Los Angeles to Sydney, Seoul or Bangkok. Although Airbus successfully aimed at this market with the A340, making sales to airlines such as All Nippon, Cathay Pacific and Singapore Airlines, it did not have the field to itself. McDonnell Douglas was a notable rival, having already produced one very good long range aircraft in the DC-10-30. After several years of indecision, the company finally launched a successor in the shape of the McDonnell Douglas MD-11 in 1985. This was a derivative of the DC-10 with a lengthened fuselage seating up to 405 passengers combined with a revised wing design, other aerodynamic refinements, an advanced two-crew flightdeck and new generation high thrust turbofans. Production aircraft were offered with either three 60,000lb thrust Pratt & Whitney PW4460 or General Electric CF6-80C2DIF turbofans. It was initially planned to offer a version powered by Rolls-Royce Trents. This was ordered by Air Europe but the subsequent demise of the British airline terminated the plans to install this powerplant. The MD-11 first flew in January 1990 with the first delivery being made to Finnair at the end of the year after an intensive test programme. Although early aircraft suffered from a shortfall in range performance, this was eventually rectified and the standard MD-11 is capable of carrying a full payload over 6,900 miles while the MD-11ER can carry 298 passengers over a staggering 8,300 miles. The aircraft is also produced in freighter and combi versions. Although sales have been slow, with only 174 ordered to the end of 1996, there have been recent indications that the all-cargo MD-11F is beginning to make a name for itself as a better bet than the rival Boeing 747 freighter. The

MD-11F was launched by Federal Express which ordered its first aircraft as far back as 1986 and currently has 17 MD-11s in its fleet. More recently, Lufthansa Cargo announced an order in late 1996 for 12 MD-11Fs.

At one stage McDonnell Douglas proposed a larger version of the MD-11 under the designation MD-12 but this was abandoned in favour of a four-engined double-deck fuselage capable of carrying up to 700 passengers or, alternatively, around 400 over a maximum range of 8,000 miles. If this project had been launched at the time of its inception in 1992, it would now be entering service at a time when the airlines are clamouring for such an aircraft. However the company decided that the risks involved in the project were too great and it was shelved, as were later plans for a twin-engined long range MD-11 derivative known as the MD-XX. Cancellation of these projects, coupled with poor sales of the MD-11 and uncertainty over the MD-95 programme, caused McDonnell Douglas problems and, in an unexpected move at the end of 1996, it was announced that McDonnell Douglas would merge with Boeing. This effectively left only one major US civil airliner manufacturer which in turn would have only one major rival, the European Airbus consortium.

By contrast Boeing's star was riding high with the introduction of most recent contender in the long haul stakes, the Boeing 777 twin-jet which weighs in between the smaller 767 and the larger four-engined 747. Originally starting life as a stretch of the Boeing 767, after consultation with several influential airlines Boeing realised that an entirely new design was required and the 777 programme was officially launched in October 1990 with the maiden flight in June 1994. Deliveries to United Airlines were made in mid-1996 while British Airways received its first aircraft later in the year. The basic production version is the 777-200 which can seat between 305 and 440 passengers and is powered by two of the latest generation high thrust turbofans. These can be General Electric GE90s, Pratt & Whitney PW4077s or Rolls-Royce Trent 877s, all in the 72 -85,000lb thrust bracket, the most powerful engines ever fitted to a civil airliner. As a twin-jet, the Boeing 777 needed to gain ETOPS approval if it were to be commercially acceptable, and Boeing went to great lengths in the test programme, which involved almost 7,000 flying hours, to ensure that the first aircraft delivered to customer airlines were so certificated – the first time that this had been done with a new aircraft as the necessary approval was normally only forthcoming after extensive in-service experience. Despite being the latest airliner in service, Boeing is already offering developments and derivatives. While the basic aircraft can carry a full payload over 5,600 miles, the latest IGW (Increased Gross Weight) version will reach out to 8,000 miles. A high capacity 777-300 is expected to be in service with Cathay Pacific in 1998 following a first flight in October 1997 and this stretched version will carry between 368 and 394 passengers while the smaller 777-100X, not yet formally launched, will be an ultra long range version capable of ranges in excess of 9,200 miles. The -300 model is seen as a natural replacement for the hundreds of classic 747 models (100/200/300), some of which will soon be 20 years old. Already 281 Boeing 777s have been sold and with McDonnell Douglas out of the running, the future of large airliner construction is firmly left to Airbus and Boeing.

At the moment Airbus has launched the new and massive A3XX in order to ensure that its product range competes across the board with Boeing, the American company previously having a monopoly at the top end of the market with the ubiquitous 747. In launching the A3XX, Airbus has to face the fact that Boeing's rival 747 derivatives will inevitably be available to customer airlines at an earlier date than the 2003 forecast for its own aircraft. However Airbus maintains that there are significant advantages in the all-new design which will offer seat/mile costs at least 15 percent lower than the best available today. A double-deck fuselage layout was chosen in order to keep overall length within criteria acceptable at today's airports and the wingspan is kept to less than 80m for the same reason. The initial A3XX-100 will be powered by four 72-78,000lb/320-347kN thrust engines to be built by

General Electric, Pratt & Whitney or Rolls-Royce (Trent 900) and will have a range of between 7,500 and 8,500 miles depending on payload, which can include up to 16 tonnes of cargo in addition to passengers, and engine type. Maximum take-off weight will be a massive 1,100,000lb and passenger capacity will be 555 in a three-class layout or over 800 in one-class economy configuration. Difficult as it is to envisage these figures, Airbus is also offering a stretched A3XX-200 which will further reduce seat/mile costs and will seat up to 990 passengers in all economy seating – 550 on the main deck and a further 450 on the upper deck. In addition the two-deck layout holds out the potential of a super combi freighter carrying around 400 passengers on the upper deck and a substantial cargo payload on a specially strengthened main deck. Airbus forecasts a market for 1,380 airliners of 500 seats and above by the year 2014 and with the A3XX it is determined to take a substantial share of the $300 billion which this implies.

For many years several airlines have been pushing for a further development of the 747 family and, spurred on by the rival Airbus proposals, Boeing responded in September 1996 with the launch of the new 500X and 600X series which will be powered by four 76,000-78,000lb thrust GE/Pratt & Whitney JV1 or Rolls-Royce RB211-Trent 976 turbofans. Both versions feature a redesigned wing and a heavier maximum take-off weight but the 500X is only slightly larger than the preceding 747-400 and its main advantage is a significant increase in range. However most interest lies in the larger 747-600X which could, for example, carry

The Boeing 777 was designed to fit between the 747 and 767. Over 150 aircraft had been ordered by the time flight testing began. It entered service with United and British Airways in 1996. With airlines like Air France replacing orders for the 767 or 737 with the 777 its future seems secure. Indeed, less than a year after its first delivery Boeing was working on its 50th aircraft and announced in autumn 1996 that production would be increasing from five to seven units a month in July 1997.

around 530 passengers in a three-class layout non-stop from Hong Kong to Los Angeles against known prevailing headwinds. This version is 48ft longer than the 747-400 and will have a take-off gross weight of 1,186,000lb. The new 747s will draw heavily on experience gained with the Boeing 777, including cabin interiors and flightdeck systems. The undercarriage is considerably modified to support the significant increase in maximum weight, the nosegear having four wheels and the other main gear bogies will carry six instead of four wheels. Boeing's great advantage in the sales war with Airbus is that its aircraft can be in service by the year 2000, three years ahead of its rival and this will be a significant factor as far as many airlines are concerned. However the 747-600X only offers a 10 percent improvement in seat/mile costs, not as much as the Airbus product, and the situation is by no means cut and dried. It is not beyond the bounds of possibility that airlines will order the 747-600X as an interim measure and subsequently place further orders for the A3XX when it matures in the future.

These giant new airliners show just how far commercial air transport has progressed in 80 years. Those intrepid passengers who sat in the wicker seats of the converted DH4 bomber, about to set off on a three or four-hour uncomfortable flight from London to Paris in 1919, could not have envisaged in their wildest dreams the prodigious advances which would be made in the following decades. They would have no idea that an airliner could fly non-stop halfway around the world, carrying hundreds of passengers in great comfort and safety at undreamed of altitudes and speeds. They would not even have thought that the aeroplane would replace the majestic ocean liner or even rival the train on much shorter journeys. It is therefore sobering to consider what may happen in the next 80 years. What appears to be sheer fantasy today could well be everyday fact in a few decades. For example, the pioneering Concorde has remained the only viable supersonic transport but a replacement must come in the next two decades. Beyond that, there have been plans for an airborne vehicle which will operate on the fringes of space while the spaceship airliner, prematurely forecast in the classic film 2001 may yet become reality. Indeed one Japanese company is already planning a commercial spacecraft which will offer fare paying passengers the chance to view the planet Earth from the remote distance of space. A slight drawback is that the fare will be $1 million for each passenger, but even at that price there will probably be enough customers to make a viable project. Who can tell where this will lead?

RIGHT: Swissair McDonnell Douglas DC-10-30 HB-IHA seen in July 1975.

80 Years of Civil Aviation:
the Aircraft

Pre World War 2

MAIN PICTURE: Travel Air Model 5000. This was a five-place cabin monoplane and was the first aircraft to be built to airline specifications. It became the first unit of the National Air Transport fleet operating both day and night between Chicago and Dallas.

INSET: The single-engined Fokker FVII was transformed by the addition of two wing-mounted 200hp Wright Whirlwind radial engines. So reliable were the FVII-3m trimotors (a FVIIa is illustrated here) that they were produced under licence all over Europe and in the USA and were used on many adventurous flights. For example, the Dutch carrier KLM was able to fly them from Amsterdam to the Dutch East Indies – a journey of nearly 10,000 miles.

TRAVEL AIR
TRANSPORT

№ 21

NAT

U.S. MAIL
EXPRESS

MAIN PICTURE: A splendid closeup of the business end of a KLM Fokker FXVIII about to start off on a mail trip. Today KLM – Koninklijke Luchvaart Maatschappij, Royal Dutch Airlines – is the oldest operating airline in the world and has been a significant force in aviation history since its founding on 7 October 1919. Granted the prefix 'Royal' by Queen Wilhelmina, KLM's history from 1919 to 1953, when he died, was linked to its founder: Albert Plesman, a Dutch Air Force officer. KLM was always closely involved with Fokker and bought many of that company's aircraft. Five FXVIIIs were built for KLM in 1932.

ABOVE: The FVII was built in the USA in modified form as the FX and FXa. Here, as the writing on the nose proudly exclaims, is an 'F-TEN A SUPER-TRIMOTOR' of Rio Grande, about to embark passengers.

BELOW: A view taken in the Smithsonian Institution's National Air and Space Museum in Washington. In the foreground Ford 4-AT Trimotor N9683; behind it Douglas DC-3 N18124 of Eastern Air Lines and a Boeing 247D; to the right, a Pitcairn Mailwing and Northrop Alpha.

A classic of the period, the Ford Trimotor first flew in 1926: 40 years later examples of the type were still flying. Nearly 200 of two main variants, the 4-AT and 5-AT; were built. Up to 11 passengers could be carried at 107mph over 500 miles. The Boeing 247D could carry 10 passengers at over 150mph and first flew in 1933. 13 were built out of a total of 75 247s. The Northrop Alpha was an important aircraft, although fewer than 20 were built. It was an all metal, stressed-skin low-wing cantilever transport monoplane which could carry eight (inc pilot).

MAIN PICTURE and INSET: Two views of the Junkers Ju52 – D-CIAK at Düsseldorf airport in October 1990 and D-TABX with swastika and red cross markings. The last Junkers aircraft to use a corrugated metal skin, the Ju52 could carry 15-17 passengers. At one time accounting for 75 percent of the Lufthansa fleet, it would serve in every theatre of WW2.

BELOW: The Boeing 247 was based on the Model 200 Monomail and Model 215. An all-metal low-wing monoplane with retractable main undercarriage, it was powered by two 550hp Pratt & Whitney radials and could carry 10 passengers about 500 miles. It had two main drawbacks: the main wing spar was an obstruction in the cabin and its performance in hot and high conditions left a lot to be desired. Its performance was enhanced in the 247D version (see previous page) and it proved a successful aircraft with United Airlines which used them until they were taken into USAF service in 1942. The 247 could well have proved more successful had Boeing's production line been capable of faster production as TWA tried to buy the aircraft. In the end UA's order had to be fulfilled and so TWA plumped for the DC-2.

The de Havilland DH83 Fox Moth first flew in January 1932. Capable of carrying four passengers, it was powered by 120hp Gipsy III of 130hp or 145hp Gipsy Major engines and was capable of a cruising speed of about 90mph. 146 were built in the UK, Australia and Canada with the latter designated DH83C. These had a pilot's canopy and, occasionally, skis or floats.

ABOVE LEFT: DH83C Fox Moth G-AOJH at Hurn in July 1987.

ABOVE: DH83 Fox Moth G-ADHA.

From 1932 just over 200 de Havilland DH84 Dragons of two main marks (I and II) were built, 87 of these in Australia in 1942-3 as RAusAF radio and navigation trainers. Capable of carrying six passengers at a cruising speed of 110mph (improved to 10 passengers at 114mph in the Mark II), the Dragon – originally the Dragon Moth – was designed to answer the need for a larger aircraft than the Fox Moth and to meet a Royal Iraqi Air Force requirement. (The eight Iraqi aircraft were designated DH83M.) The Dragon proved cheap to to operate and easy to maintain.

LEFT: Aer Lingus DH84 Dragon EI-ABI, named Iolar, at Bristol in July 1986.

RIGHT and BELOW: Initially known as the Dragon Six, the DH89 Dragon Rapide saw both commercial and military use. While many civil Rapides were taken into RAF service during WW2, there was also a dedicated military version – the DH89M, called the Dominie in RAF service. Continued production up to 1945 saw over 700 produced and their ease of maintenance, low operating costs and simple construction contributed to their longevity.

FAR RIGHT and INSET: The Lockheed 10 Electra also saw much US military use in four versions. In total 148 were built, most of them 10As – although there were three other main versions, the B, C and E.

BOTTOM RIGHT: The DH90 Dragonfly was designed as a private tourer – although it did see service with many airlines.

The Douglas DC-3 was, quite simply, the classic propliner of all time. The most widely used civil or military airliner and transport, it still continues on in commercial service some 60 years after its first flight in 1935. Born out of a sleeper version of the DC-2, the DC-3 was exquisitely aerodynamic and became so ubiquitous that it was always said that the only replacement for a DC-3 . . . was another DC-3. Taking this to extremes, a number of companies have produced turboprop versions of the DC-3 – the first was in the UK using Armstrong Whitworth Mambas. Currently the US Basler Corporation produces the T-67 and South African Professional Aviation the Jet Prop DC-3 AMI; both have P&W Canada PT6 turboprops.

Here a variety of DC-3s are pictured: Southern International's G-AMCA in January 1977 (ABOVE LEFT); Budget Rent a Plane's HI-445 at Fort Lauderdale in March 1988 (INSET); Northwest's G-AMPY at North Weald in May 1986 (LEFT); Eastern Express's N34PB (ABOVE); and N660JB of Air Adventures in April 1988 (RIGHT).

More views of the DC-3, capturing the continued interest in this much loved workhorse.

MAIN PICTURE: The DC-3 was modified to take skis and floatplanes. Perhaps the best-known event associated with the former was Operation 'High Jump', an Antarctic expedition by the USN which included use of carrier-launched R4D-5s (81 C-47As intended for USAAF use were transferred to the USN with this designation) equipped with jet-assisted take-off rockets and skis. The floatplane version was the C-47C which was equipped with Edo floats. These carried 300 US gal of fuel and had retractable wheels. Here Floatplane N130Q is seen in May 1993.

ABOVE RIGHT: Airshow duties for this gleaming DC-3.

FAR RIGHT: Air Atlantique began charter work with DC-3s in 1977. It now operates nine DC-3s for both pleasure and business as shown here: an Air Atlantique DC-3 at an airshow at Eindhoven in July 1985. It is painted with a Dakota 50th anniversary logo. The first DC-3 flight was on 17 December 1935 – coincidentally 32 years to the day after the first manned flight by the Wright Brothers at Kittyhawk, North Carolina.

BELOW: Used for oil spillage duties, Air Atlantique's 'Pollution Control' G-AMCA is still going strong today.

THIS PAGE: Using the same engines as the Model 10 Electra, with a top speed of 225mph at 5,000ft, in 1936 the Model 12 Electra Junior won a Bureau of Air \this use that most of the 130 Model 12s built between 1936 and 1942 were destined. The bulk of the production run was sold either to military customers – including the RAF – or to private operators, including 36 aircraft to the US or foreign governments. Here three views of Lockheed 12 NC-18137 at Tico in March 1988.

ABOVE RIGHT: The Short Mayo composite aircraft was formed of a modified Empire class flying boat Maia and the smaller Mercury on top. The first separation took place in 1938 but the idea didn't prove economic.

BELOW RIGHT and FOLLOWING PAGE: The Grumman G-21 Goose: most of the 250+ built went originally to the military – especially the USN and US Coast Guard – although postwar they were sold into the civil market.

Post World War 2

ABOVE LEFT: More than 9,000 of the Beechcraft Model 18 were built between 1937 and 1969. The majority were military versions: it saw use with the USAAF, as the UC-45, the USN (JRB), RAF and RN (Expediter I and II). Other developments included the AT-7 Navigator and AT-11 Kansas trainer. Here an Expediter of British Caribbean Airways in November 1982.

ABOVE: The Grumman G-44 Widgeon saw the bulk of its 200+ production run bought by the USN; 40 were built by SCAN in France. As with its stablemate, the G-21 Goose, the G-44 was modified postwar to produce up-engined versions, McKinnon converting many into Super Widgeons with 300hp Lycoming engines.

LEFT: The Avro 685 York was a derivation of the Lancaster, whose wings, engine, tail and undercarriage were used. Over 250 were built with production ending in 1948. It could carry up to 65 passengers with a crew of four. This is ex-RAF MW100 at Cosford Museum in May 1985.

With a standard single tailplane as opposed to triple fins and a gross design weight of 50,000lb as against over 60,000lb, the DC-4 redesign was a completely different aircraft to the original prototype DC-4 which was redesignated DC-4E (for experimental). When the war intervened, the DC-4 became the C-54 Skymaster and served with distinction as military transport for the USAAF, USN and, in small numbers under Lend-Lease, the RAF. As well as notable wartime work they were the mainstay of the US contribution to the 1948 Berlin Airlift and continued on in the military service of a number of countries following their disposal as surplus by the US military air arms.

The first commercial operator was American Export Airlines who flew DC-4s across the Atlantic from Gander to Shannon and Hurn, the first landplane service to do this. The DC-4 airframe proved so successful that it was stretched first to become the DC-6 and then the DC-7. Today DC-4s still fly, mainly in the freighter role in South America; some are also used as water bombers (as illustrated FAR RIGHT).

ABOVE: The Short Solent was the civil version of the S45 Seaford, the development of the Sunderland destined for Pacific Theatre use. Too late for WW2 a Seaford was trialled by BOAC and performed well enough to lead to an order of 12. Capable of carrying 34 passengers in some style, the Solent 1 saw three upgradings, the Solent 4 carrying 44 passengers.

RIGHT: The Short Sandringham was a conversion of the military transport version of the Sunderland – the maritime patrol and reconaissance flying boat. Various marks of Sandringham were built, 26 aircraft in total. They remained in service up to the 1960s.

TOP and LEFT: On 25 September 1945 the prototype de Havilland DH104 Dove became the first new civil transport to fly after WW2. It went on to become an outstanding success, with over 540 built. The final version, the Dove 8, cruised at around 200mph with a range of over 800 miles. The last aircraft left the production line in 1967. The Dove was used by the RAF (as the Devon C1) and the RN (as the Devon C20). Modification in the US led to the Riley Turbo-Exec 400, which had swept tail and fins and 400hp Lycomings (as opposed to the Dove 8's Gipsy Queens; see TOP photograph), and the Texas Airplane CJ600, a stretched version which could seat 18.

The Lockheed Constellation – the 'Queen of the Airways' – was one of the most beautiful propliners ever built and, at the time it entered commercial service after WW2, one of the most advanced. Designed to meet a TWA requirement for a pressurised 40-passenger airliner, the prototype flew on 9 January 1943, after the USA entered the war. The earliest aircraft, therefore (15 of an intended requirement for 180), went to the USAAF as the C-69. A further military version – the C-121 – would be based on the Model 749. 233 Connies would be built, the final aircraft – a Model 749A – being delivered in September 1951.

Constellations were sold as new to many airlines including BOAC, TWA, Pan Am, American Overseas Airlines, KLM, Air France, Air India, Eastern, Aer Linte, Qantas, South African Airlines, Avianca and Chicago and Southern. They would continue in service for many years, well into 1980s.

OPPOSITE PAGE
TOP: An L749 Constellation on a wet day in February 1978.

CENTRE: F-ZVMV was an L749, c/n 2503, originally registered NC86520 and company-owned. It was sold to Aerovias Guest and Air France before being bought by the French Armée de l'Air in 1962. It was used as an engine testbed until it went to the Musée de l'Air, at Le Bourget.

BELOW and THIS PAGE: Three views of L749A HI421 of Aerochago SA at San Juan Airport, Puerto Rico, March 1988. The L749A had a strengthened structure to give an improved maximum take-off weight of 107,000lb as against 102,000lb for the L749; there were 59 L749As constructed and many L749s were converted by using kits. A number of the L749s were – as here – fitted with strengthened floors for extra weight and a freight door. This one is at the rear; others were forward.

The Douglas Corporation realised that the competition in the commercial aircraft market in the immediate postwar years would be intense. The DC-4, produced in numbers for military use, would not compete against the pressurised and more technically advanced competitors like the Constellation. An improved DC-4 was needed – a sensible view that was proved right: 79 DC-4s were sold to airlines as against 704 of the DC-6 family.

Having started life on the military C-54 Skymaster replacement programme, the first DC-6s reached American Airlines and United Air Lines in November 1946. They were pressurised and stretched DC-4s with improved payload and performance. Subsequently they too were stretched and upgraded to DC-6A and DC-6B standard.

The DC-6 proved long-lived and an admirable workhorse; in the mid-1990s there were still over 100 DC-6s in operation – often as freighters. This was a far cry from the difficult days of 1947 when the DC-6 fleet was grounded because of fuselage fires.

The photographs on this spread show a variety of DC-6s including (BELOW) a DC-6BF of Trans-Air-Link. As with many aircraft the DC-6Bs were used as freighters after their passenger carrying days were over. Identified as DC-6BFs, they had reinforced floors and cargo doors.

The Boeing 377 Stratocruiser was derived from the B-29 Superfortress programme, producing a pressurised long-range aircraft which could cruise at 340mph to a range of 2,750 miles. Its military designation was C-97 and in this form was the mainstay of US military transport squadrons during the 1950s.

Only 55 Boeing 377s were built: it wasn't liked by the airlines mainly because of its P&W Wasp Major engines – but also because of the advent of new jet types onto the market.

The Stratocruisers and C-97s saw considerable service through the secondhand market and there were also a number of conversions including those by the Israeli Air Industry; the KC-97 tankers for the USAF and the amazing Guppies and Super Guppies, used mainly by NASA, which gave a 54,000lb payload potential.

ABOVE and ABOVE LEFT: Military KC-97 tankers.

LEFT: Boeing C-97 of Agro Air Inc seen in Miami, March 1988.

The
1950s

LEFT and ABOVE LEFT: Grumman was the leading US producer of amphibians and flying boats with a range that included the Duck, Goose, Widgeon and – as illustrated here – the Mallard.

ABOVE: The Convair 240/340/440 family of medium range transports were designed to be C-47 replacements. With production figures of 176, 311 (including nearly 100 for the military) and 179 respectively, they were a successful and long-lived family, many of which (about 230 examples) were converted into turboprops between 1955 and 1967. A 240 is illustrated.

RIGHT: Another DC-3 'replacement', the Martin 4-0-4 was the last in a family that, like the Convair series, was a response to American Airlines' specification for a medium-range airliner. The 2-0-2 (43 built) in August 1947 became the first postwar twin to be given type approval by the Civil Aeronautics Authority; the pressurised and stretched 4-0-4 saw a production run of 103.

ABOVE and RIGHT: The Constellation was improved over its life and max gross weight had increased from 90,000lb to 107,000lb without any major structural change. In the competitive commercial aviation world of the 1950s, as Douglas, Boeing and Lockheed vied for market share, it wasn't long before the constant search for improvement led to such a change, the Constellation being stretched by nearly 20ft by adding two fuselage sections fore and aft of the wing spars. The resulting L1049 Super Constellation would have a production run of 579, a good number of which went to the USN and USAF as early warning and electronic reconnaissance aircraft. Designated mainly WV-2 or EC-121, until a land-based chain of radar stations took over in 1965, the USAF Early Warning squadrons were responsible for AEW over the North Atlantic.

The Super Constellation was a graceful aircraft and, in its Model 1049G – 'Super G' – form, an extremely powerful one, capable of a gross weight of 137,000lb, a range of over 4,000 miles and a cruising speed at 20,000ft of over 300mph.

RIGHT and BELOW RIGHT: The de Havilland DH114 was a DH104 Dove replacement; called the Heron it first flew in 1950 and was produced in two main versions – the Mk 1 which had a fixed tricycle undercarriage and the Mk 2 whose undercarriage was retractable. A total of 148 Herons was built and the rights to the design were acquired by Saunders Aircraft of Canada. This company was to produce converted versions of the Heron as the ST-27, with a stretched fuselage increasing seating from 17 to 23 and P&W PT6A turboprops, and the ST-28, with more fuel capacity, an improved interior and redesigned tail. Other companies produced turboprop Herons, including Shin Meiwa of Japan (the Tawron), Riley (the Turbo-Skyliner) and Executive Air Engineering. A turboprop-engined version, Prinair N570PR, is seen taxying (BELOW RIGHT).

RIGHT: De Havilland Aircraft of Canada, originally part of the de Havilland group and, after 1974, part of Hawker Siddeley, started to design a range of successful light aircraft, the first being the DHC-1 Chipmunk which became the RCAF and RAF's primary trainer. The DHC-2 Beaver was designed to meet the STOL requirements of the rugged Canadian wilderness, often needing floats or skis. Tough and reliable, capable of carrying seven passengers, it found favour with both the US (968 bought) and British Army (46); other air arms followed suit. A Turbo-Beaver was introduced in 1963 with a P&W PT6A turboprop.

CENTRE RIGHT: SA Twin Pioneer.

BELOW RIGHT: The de Havilland DHA-3 Drover was designed and built by the DH Australian subsidiary to replace the DH84 Dragon. The need for good performance in rugged conditions put a heavy emphasis on STOL capability. The Drover was a fixed-undercarriage tri-motor using much of the DH104 Dove's structural features and could carry eight passengers.

OPPOSITE PAGE: The Comet's chequered history began with the first Brabazon Committee's recommendation for a jet-powered tailless aircraft for transatlantic mail routes. The resulting airliner became the first jet to enter commercial service in May 1952 and quickly halved flight times and provided high altitude pressurised comfort of a level never seen before. In 1958 the first Comet 4, a stretched, 63-81-seater incorporating all the technical and structural results of the crash investigation, took to the air. The Comet 4C airframe formed the basis of the RAF's Nimrod maritime recce and ASW aircraft.

ABOVE: Dan-Air was the last operator of civil Comets, here a 4, G-APDB which was bought by the EAAS and is preserved at Duxford.

BELOW: XS235 Canopus, an RAF Comet 4C.

The Douglas DC-7 was the final derivative of the DC-4 family, and the last of Douglas's piston-engined commercial aircraft – a response to the Super Constellation. 3ft 4in longer than the DC-6B, the 7C – the so called 'Seven Seas' – was the top version which first flew in December 1955. It had a 10ft increase in wingspan, could carry up to 105 passengers over 4,000 miles at over 300mph at 20,000ft – very similar figures to its Lockheed rival. Subsequently many of the DC-7Cs were converted to freighters and remained in service into the 1980s.

336 DC-7s were produced, with sales to all the major airlines – American, Delta, Eastern, Pan Am, United, SAA, Swissair, BOAC, Sabena, KLM, Alitalia, Japan Air Lines, etc.

One of the milestones in aviation history – the Vickers Viscount was the first turboprop-powered aircraft to enter commercial scheduled service on 18 April 1953. 444 Viscounts were produced, making it one of Britain's most successful civil aircraft – with the added bonus of selling well to US operators, another British first. It had started eight years earlier with the Brabazon Committee which identified the need for high-speed transports for European routes. The resulting Type 630 – it would have been called Viceroy rather than Viscount had the partition of India not taken place in 1947 – was underpowered and smaller than the production 700 series, which used Rolls-Royce RDa6 Dart turbo-props; passenger capacity increased to 53. The stretched 800 series (as illustrated) could carry a bigger payload of up to 75 passengers.

The ultimate stretching of the Constellation was the L1649A Starliner, 44 of which were built and sold as new to TWA, Air France and Lufthansa. Designed to compete with the DC-7C and entering service on 1 June 1957, the Starliner mated a new wing with the Super Constellation's fuselage and tail.

It was all to no avail: within a few months the jet-powered 707 and Comet 4 would render all long-distance piston-engined aircraft if not obsolete, then certainly lagging behind the field. Lockheed stopped production, well out of pocket, and the Starliners were relegated to secondary, freight or – quite successfully – to the charter business.

These views are of N974R of Maine Coast Airways at Fort Lauderdale.

Fokker has been a great name in the industry since the earliest days and it is hardly surprising that the company's first postwar offering was as successful and clever as any it had produced before. Having spent the immediate postwar years refurbishing ex-military DC-3s to civil standards, it is also not surprising that Fokker plumped for a similar, piston-engined aircraft as its first postwar product.

Co-produced with a US licencing agreement with Fairchild of Maryland – who later became Fairchild-Hiller – the F27 Friendship (F-27 and, later, FH-227 in the USA) was produced in large numbers – 786 of all types (205 in the US) with sales to over 150 customers in more than 60 countries. Military versions – mainly the Dutch-built F27 Mk 400 Troopship for the RNethAF and maritime patrol aircraft – were also produced and many of the type are still in service today.

From 30 to 60 passengers were carried in a variety of marks including stretched versions like the F27 Mk 500 and FH-227 and freighter versions.

Today, with its hugely successful range of airliners – 727, 737, 747, 757, 767, 777 – and its run of military aircraft – B-17, B-29, B-47, B-52, KC-97, KC-135, E-3, E-4 – it is easy to think that the 'Planemaker to the World' has always held its position of dominance. In fact, before the 707 it was Douglas and Lockheed that ruled the commercial long-haul skies. The Boeing 707 changed all that. The production line started rolling in 1957; the first production aircraft flew on 20 December and the aircraft would stay in production until the line was finally closed in 1992.

By that time the aircraft had developed from the 707-100 to the 707-300C, a cargo/passenger combi of which 337 were built.

The Douglas DC-8 – known today as the McDonnell Douglas DC-8 following the merger of the two companies in 1967 – was a radical departure from the company's DC-4/6/7 family. Finally convinced that the turbojet was the future – partly because of Boeing's 367-80 prototype which would become the 707 – Douglas started working on the DC-8.

The plan was very similar to Boeing's: swept wings (although not as swept), four underslung turbojets and typical mixed class passenger accommodation for about 125. Unfortunately, while initial support from Pan Am, Eastern, KLM, JAL, National, SAS and United kept pace with 707 orders, from the end of 1956 the DC-8 was always struggling to keep up with its more flexibly configured rival. So substantial was this discrepancy that in 1965 Douglas announced its decision to vary from its fixed airframe parameters and produce the Super Sixty Series – with different combinations of fuselage tied into differing payload, range and engine possibilities. Sales doubled and by the time production ceased in May 1972, 556 had been built. The final, DC-8-63 version, could carry up to 259 passengers at a max cruising speed just short of 600mph.

Following cessation of production, 110 DC-8-60s were reengined with CFM56 turbofans by Cammacorp (as illustrated on Delta's N825E – MAIN PICTURE).

ABOVE: The Handley Page Herald was yet another DC-3 replacement which didn't work. Originally planned with four piston engines it was finally put into production with two Rolls-Royce Dart turboprops. 50 had been built before the demise of the company stopped production: very few of them remain flying today.

CENTRE RIGHT: F-BHRI was called Bretagne in Air France service.

BELOW RIGHT: F-GATZ was built in 1964 and bought by Minerve in 1978.

The Caravelle's claim to fame was that it was the world's first short to medium range turbojet-powered airliner. Built to a French government requirement, it was financed by the government and 46 of the 282 built were bought by Air France. Manufacture was by the state-owned SNCASE which merged with SNCASO to form Sud Aviation. Sud in turn merged with Nord to become Aérospatiale. The final model was the Caravelle 12, a stretched version which could carry up to 140 passengers. It first flew on 29 October 1970 and production ceased in 1973.

ABOVE and LEFT: For the Lockheed L188 Electra – like the Comet – the story is very much about what might have been rather than what actually happened. A brilliant design that could outperform jets – with none of the noise restriction problems – its career halted after a series of unexplained crashes led to an FAA maximum cruising speed restriction. The fault found, Lockheed embarked on a $25 million Lockheed Electra Achievement Program which solved the problem: but it was too late. Public confidence was lost and, anyway, jets were the fashionable way to cover medium range services. It would only be later when fuel consumption and noise levels became important that the Electra's performance would be seen for what it was. Production ceased at 170 – a figure much lower than its military derivative for the USN, the P-3 Orion ASW and maritime reconnaissance aircraft.

LEFT: The Ilyushin Il-18 is similar in role to the Electra and was produced in substantial numbers for eastern bloc usage. Code-named 'Coot' by NATO, the Il-18 could carry up to 125 passengers.

The 1960s

ABOVE: The 880 was Convair's entry into the jet airliner market. Only 65 were built and the design was blown out of the water by Boeing's 720 – a lighter and smaller version of the 707.

RIGHT and BELOW RIGHT: 230 members of the Convair 240/340/440 family were converted from piston to turboprop power, designated 580, 600 and 640. This was a very successful programme, as the numbers suggest. The 580s had two 3,750shp Allison 501-D13H turboprops; the conversion work on 130 aircraft was done by Pacific Airmotive from 1960 onwards. Illustrated are 580s of Prinair and United Express.

TOP RIGHT: The Convair 990A Coronado was a development of the Convair 880 and encountered difficulties during flight testing: this led to costly – and time consuming – modifications. This did not help an airliner already suffered from scompetition by Boeing. In the end only 37 were built and most of these ended up with the Spanish charter company Spantax, whose EC-BZO is illustrated here.

RIGHT and BELOW: The Boeing 720 – 154 were produced of this short to medium range version of the 707. Reduced fuselage length, lighter engines, reduced fuel capacity and weight savings in undercarriage and skin thicknesses all contributed to a maximum take-off weight of around 230,000lb – as against the 707-320C's 334,000lb.

FAR RIGHT and MAIN PICTURE: The Canadair CL-44 was developed from the Bristol 170 Freighter; a large turboprop it was designed to meet an RCAF trooper/freighter requirement announced in 1956. 12 CC-106 Yukons (as they were called) were built and served until the early 1970s when they were sold as freighters. In total 27 CL-44s were built.

BOTTOM RIGHT: Conway Aircraft converted one CL-44D to become the only CL-44-O – a Guppy-style transport with a double-bubble fuselage. It retained the hinged tail of the CL-44D-4s.

OPPOSITE PAGE: The Vickers Vanguard was a larger version of the Viscount – all-new but similar in style to the Viscount and powered by four Rolls-Royce Tyne 512 turboprops. It appeared on the market just as the short/medium-range airliners were moving towards jet power – as with the Caravelle and DC-9 and BAC One-Eleven. Only 43 were built.

ABOVE LEFT: The Argosy – originated as an Armstrong Whitworth design and built by Hawker Siddeley – was limited by its short range (485 miles with max payload) and operating costs. 56 went to the RAF and 17 into commercial service.

CENTRE LEFT: The Aviation Traders ATL-98 Carvair was a DC-4 conversion designed to carry up to five cars: 21 DC-4s were changed.

BELOW LEFT: The DHC-4 Caribou originated as a twin-engined version of the Otter. US and Canadian Army interest led to a larger aircraft with good military sales.

THIS PAGE: The HS748 was started by Avro before it was subsumed first into the Hawker Siddeley Group and then into British Aerospace in 1977. 349 were built in the UK and under licence by Hindustan Aeronautics Ltd. The 31 military versions for the RAF were called the Andover. The first 748s were the Series 1 followed by Series 2, 2A (RIGHT), 2B (BELOW RIGHT) and the Super 748 which could carry up to 58 passengers to a range of just over 1,000 miles.

FAR RIGHT: A Fairchild FH-227 of DAT – Delta Air Lines – of Belgium. Today a subsidiary of SABENA and flying scheduled services, DAT started in 1966 as an air taxi/charter company using DC-3s.

RIGHT and BELOW RIGHT: The Britten-Norman Islander started as a private venture between John Britten and Desmond Norman, who had learnt their trade at the de Havilland Technical School. They set up on the Isle of Wight and the Islander prototype – the BN-2 (BN-1 was an unsuccessful aircraft called the Finibee) – flew in 1965. Financial difficulties saw first Fairey and the Pilatus take over the project which was later produced as a trimotor (the Trislander) and for the military as the Defender. Over 1,200 have been built.

BELOW: The Beech 90 King Air was developed from the piston-engined Queen Air. It first flew in 1964 and in 1969 a King Air 100 was introduced.

OPPOSITE PAGE: The Trident was proposed to meet a BEA requirement for a short-haul jet. The DH121 was announced the winner in 1958. It was unusual for having three rear-mounted engines, and was the first airliner capable of full all-weather operation using blind-landing equipment. The final version was the Trident 3, stretched to take up to 180 passengers and had a Rolls-Royce RB162-86 in the tail. Illustrated are: Trident 1C (TOP), Trident 2E (CENTRE) and Trident 3B (BOTTOM).

The Boeing 727 – until overtaken by its stablemate the 737 – was the west's most produced jet airliner. Over 1,800 were built between 9 February 1963 (first flight of United's N7001U, the first off the line) and 28 August 1984 (first flight of N217FE, Federal Express's 727-2S2F, the last). The 727 came in three main versions – the -100, the stretched -200 and the -200 Advanced, the latter using P&W JT8D-15 engines which gave 50 percent more range and an increase in max take-off weight to 191,000lb allowing it to carry up to 189 passengers just under 3,000 miles at 570mph at 30,000ft. Late in the production run, Boeing built 15 -200Fs freight aircraft for Federal Express. Since the end of the run, the 727 has been reengined both to improve performance and also to reduce noise levels. The two main concerns to do this were Valsan (just over 20 727-200s) and Dee Howard of San Antonio, Texas, who modified 40 727-100s for UPS. This modification included reengining with Rolls-Royce Tay 651-54 turbofans and upgrade of the cockpit instrumentation.

LEFT: The VC10 was a handsome airliner, which originated at the Vickers Armstrong Weybridge works. Produced by BAC, 32 standard and 22 Super VC10s were built as well 14 for the RAF. Subsequently, the RAF converted airliners into tankers. This photograph shows ZA141, (originally BOAC's G-ARVG) and ZA148 (originally SY-ADA of East African Airways) both were bought by the RAF in 1977.

ABOVE and BELOW: The BAC 1-11 came in six versions: the Series 200 (56 built), Srs 300 (9), Srs 400 (69), Srs 475 (9), Srs 500 (89) and, finally, Srs 560 built in Romania by Romaero as the Rombac 1-11. Retrofitting of cargo doors, reengining with Rolls-Royce Tays and hush kits for the power-plants are all still in progress.

G-AVMM (ABOVE) and G-AVMK (BELOW), both 1-11-510EDs, originally went to BEA and became part of BA on the merger in 1974. Their final owner was European AviationAir Charter at Hurn.

The DC-9 came in five main versions – the DC-9-10 (137 built), DC-9-20 (10), DC-9-30 (662), DC-9-40 (71) and DC-9-50 (96). This total of 976 of all variants started with the first flight on 25 February 1965, ending with the final delivery – a DC-9-30 to the USN on 28 October 1982.

ABOVE: Alitalia took 38 DC-9-32s in standard or freight form. This is I-DIZA originally called Isola di Palmarola, at Heathrow in 1984.

CENTRE RIGHT: Republic DC-9-15 N48075. Republic was taken over by Northwest Airlines in 1986.

BELOW RIGHT: On 26 November 1968 N9336, a DC-9-31, was one of 15 sold to Air West, later taken over by Northwest, the largest operator of DC-9s with nearly 140 on its books at one stage.

TOP RIGHT: Aeromexico took 15 DC-9-32s and acquired others, XA-JEC Ixtapa being one of them.

FAR RIGHT: DC-9-51 HB-ISV Winkel one of 38 bought as new by Swissair.

ABOVE: When the Antonov An-22 flew first in 1965 it was both the USSR's largest aircraft and also the largest in the world until superseded by the C-5 Galaxy. Code-named 'Cock' by NATO, about 50 were built up to 1974.

RIGHT: The Belfast was based on the Bristol Britannia, the military version of which had been built by Shorts. Deliveries to the RAF started in 1966. Mothballed by 1977, two were sold to Transmeridian who became HeavyLift in whose colours G-BFYU is seen.

BELOW RIGHT: Based on the Stratocruiser/C-97, eight Guppies were built – three Minis and five Supers. F-GEAI, converted by UTI in France, is a Super Guppy carrying Airbus components to Toulouse.

OPPOSITE PAGE
ABOVE: OK-OBL Ostrava, an Ilyushin Il-62M of CSA – Czech Airlines, a company which can trace its ancestry back to the 1920s. Today the Ilyushins are gone and western aircraft like 737s ply the airlanes from Prague.

CENTRE and BELOW: 725 Tupolev Tu-134s were built 1962-90 in three versions: the early Tu-134 (CENTRE); the Tu-134A (BELOW) and Tu-134B.

Well over 2,500 Boeing 737s have been sold since the first 737-100. The short/medium range airliner has proved to be long-lived and, above all, adaptable. The main variants – Series 100, 200, 300, 400 and 500 are to be joined by the 700 which is planned for 1998 delivery.

ABOVE LEFT: Bahamasair 737-200 C6-BEH was one of four bought for passenger and freight use.

BOTTOM LEFT: Britannia Airways, part of the Thomson organisation, was the first European operator of the 737-200 in 1968. At one time over 30 were on the books but they began to be phased out from the mid-1980s; the last went in 1994. Here 737-204ADV G-BECG Amy Johnson in May 1987.

ABOVE: Gulf Air, since 1974 jointly owned by the governments of Bahrain, Oman, Qatar and the UAE, acquired eight 737-200s in the late 1970s. This is A40-BC.

BELOW LEFT: Canadian Airlines International was formed in 1988 by the merger of Pacific Western and Canadian Pacific. Over 70 737s were at one stage owned by the company. This one, C-FHCP, is seen the year after the company was formed.

MAIN PICTURE: Lufthansa was the first customer for the 737 and has supported the airliner consistently since its first Srs 100 was delivered in 1967. Photo shows 737-230 D-ABFA.

British Airports

The growth of civil aviation, expansion caused by war and the quantum jump in passenger numbers in the last 30 years have had a huge impact on airports the world over: Britain is no exception. Today the need for expansion is greater than ever, but kept in check by the ecological issues of noise pollution, road and infrastructure construction.

ABOVE LEFT: A British Airways BAC 1-11 at Aberdeen. Dyce Airport has seen passengers since 1934; its major expansion took place at the end of the 1970s thanks to the oil industry.

LEFT: Birmingham Elmdon opened in 1939 and saw testing of Lancasters and Stirlings during WW2.

BELOW: BAe's test airfield at Filton, Bristol.

RIGHT: A pilot's eye view of Heathrow, looking west. This is the main complex of terminals with No 1 closest to the camera. Terminal 4, opened in 1986, is to the left, just out of shot.

BELOW RIGHT: Manchester airport has recently been chosen for substantial development.

The 1970s

ABOVE and RIGHT: The Jetstream started life as a Handley Page project – 35 were built – which was taken up by the former HP company Scottish Aviation in the mid-1960s. Produced as the Jetstream 200 a further 26 were built for the RAF. BAe took over Scottish Aviation on its inception and relaunched the aircraft as the BAe Jetstream 31 (as illustrated). This proved successful for the commuter/ feeder market and an improved version – the Super 31 – first flew on 7 October 1988. Subsequent development led to the Jetstream 41 which started production in early 1994.

ABOVE RIGHT: Britten-Norman BN-2A Mk III Trislander of Aviation West. 73 Trislanders were built in the UK. Developed from the Islander, the Trislander had a 3ft 6in lengthened fuse-lage, a capacity increase from 10 to 17 passengers and a third Textron Lycoming engine in a nacelle mounted on the tail unit. The first flight was on 11 September 1970.

OPPOSITE PAGE
ABOVE and BELOW: So successful was the F27 Friendship that Fokker decided to proceed with a short-range (c600 miles) 32-seater – and so the F28 Fellowship was born. Built by Shorts (wings), VFW and HFB in Germany (rear fuselage and tail) and Fokker, powered by Rolls-Royce Spey Mk 555 turbofans, this handsome airliner started production in the late 1960s. 241 were produced with the Mk 4000 the most successful (111 built). This variant could carry 85 passengers nearly 1,300 miles. Illustrated are 65-seat Mk 1000 models of Air France and Piedmont.

ABOVE and CENTRE LEFT: The Tupolev Tu-154 was code-named 'Careless' by NATO and was a three-engined short/medium range jet. Over 900 were built in three main versions – A, B and M – seeing service mainly with Aeroflot but also with other Soviet bloc airlines. Illustrated are LZ-BTP, a Tu-154B-1 of Balkan Bulgarian Airlines and HA-LCR, a Tu-154B-2 of Malev, the Hungarian airline.

BELOW LEFT: The LET L-410 Turbolet has been a successful light transport for its Czech builders. Over 1,000 have been delivered since production started in 1969. Illustrated is an L-410 at Farnborough.

The Boeing 747 changed the face of air travel, bringing long distance mass market flights within the spending power of a massive population. Every aspect of air travel – pricing, airport size and passenger handling capacity – had to be rethought as loads increased from the 350+ of the -100 to the -400's 550+. Illustrated on this spread are early models: Virgin Atlantic 747-243B G-VGIN Scarlet Lady (ABOVE) still flying today; TWA's 747-100 N17104 (BELOW); Wardair's 747-101 C-FFUN (BELOW LEFT); and Thai Airways International's 747-2D7B Visuthakasatriya HS-TGA, (MAIN PICTURE). The sheer age and mileage of the early 747s brings its own problems: some are nearly 30 years old!

OPPOSITE PAGE

ABOVE: A freight version – Flying Tigers' 747-249F N808FT William E Bartling.

BELOW: Air France is a major purchaser of 747s and currently has over 40. This is a 747-228B Combi, combining passenger and freight carriage to get the best of both worlds.

ABOVE LEFT: Air India 747-237B VT-EBN Emperor Rajendra Chola is seen at Paris Charles de Gaulle in 1989. Air India took possession of its first 747 in 1971. VT-EBN is still serving.

CENTRE LEFT: Pan Am had the distinction of being the first airline to put the 747 into service. It performed dreadfully! Bedevilled by engine problems, the proving flight to London was late and the first New York-London fare-paying service didn't get off the ground without a change of aircraft. Here 747-212B Clipper Cathay.

BELOW LEFT: Royal Jordanian Airlines 747-2D3B Prince Ali.

OPPOSITE PAGE and ABOVE: The Ilyushin Il-76M was the military version of this long-distance rear-loading freighter. Code-named 'Candid' by NATO, over 750 were built including 350+ for the military. However, many of the Il-76M versions went to Aeroflot – becoming Il-76MDs – and a large number still serve in these post-Communist days. The payload is 88,185lb giving a maximum take-off weight of 374,784lb. With this payload a range of 2,250+ miles can be achieved.

CENTRE and BELOW LEFT: The Antonov An-26 was a development of the An-24. Code-named 'Curl' by NATO, over 1,000 were built and many are still in service. The An-26 had a rear-loading ramp, two Ivchenko AI-24VT turboprops and could carry 38-40 passengers. It was seen first in the west at the 1969 Paris Air Show. Illustrated is CU-T1238 of Cubana.

The Lockheed L1011 TriStar was unfortunate to come into existence at a time when its parent company was in financial difficulties as was its engine manufacturer – Rolls-Royce. It was only the direct intervention of the British government that kept Rolls-Royce alive and its RB211 turbofans available.

RIGHT: Omani-registered Gulfair A40-TV started life as Eastern Air Lines' N328EA. It was converted to become a .200 in June 1982. Once the main aircraft of the Gulfair fleet from delivery in 1976, the TriStars have now made way for 767s and Airbuses.

BELOW: Pan Am TriStar 500 N505PA Clipper Eagle Wing. The 500 was a long-range version with extended wings, a shorter fuselage (which led to the loss of a port side door) and internal improvements.

ABOVE RIGHT: Air Portugal's TriStar 500 CS-TEB Infante D. Henrique was delivered in 1983.

BELOW RIGHT: Air Canada's C-FTNL was delivered in 1974 and converted to become a TriStar 100 in 1977.

TOP LEFT: DC-10 F-GDJK was delivered in 1975 as ZK-NZR for Air New Zealand by International Lease Finance Corps, it was leased to Linhas Aereas de Mocambique when this photo was taken in 1979.

MAIN PICTURE: CP Air, now part of Canadian Airlines International, and DC-10-30 C-GCPD Empress of British Colombia, *still in service, though now as* Empress of Sydney.

BOTTOM LEFT: Northwest DC-10.

ABOVE: Lufthansa's D-ADJO Essen, a DC-10-30.

LEFT: American Airlines' N123AA, a DC-10-10.

ABOVE and CENTRE RIGHT: The Brazilian EMBRAER EMB-110 Bandeirante started production in the late 1960s as a military light transport: 500 were built by the time production ceased in 1990. The stretched EMB-110P1 had a rear cargo door; the EMB-110P2, which first flew in 1977, had front and back passenger doors and carried 18 passengers. IIllustrated are two EMB-110P1s – EI-BPI, originally used by Ryanair between Waterford and Gatwick, is seen in the colours of Iona National Airways; and Jersey European Airways' G-BGYV which was acquired by Business Air Travel, set up in 1985.

BELOW RIGHT: Beech Super King Air 200 – it had more powerful engines, a T-tail, lengthened fuselage and other improvements, seating 6-8 passengers. G-BRON of Executive Express in 1981.

OPPOSITE PAGE
The Airbus A300 was the start of a hugely successful European range of airliners which came closer to breaking the stranglehold of the US giants than any other type. Selling all over the globe, the twin-engined A300 is still going strong. Illustrated here are A300B4 Air France's F-BVGM (ABOVE); Pan Am's N211PA (CENTRE); and Air Jamaica's 6Y-JMK (BELOW) named Spirit of Montego Bay.

MAIN PICTURE: Veritair Beech Super King Air G-BIXM.

ABOVE LEFT and LEFT: Dassault Mercure 100s F-BTTJ and F-BTTI of Air Inter, the main French domestic airline which was set up in 1954. Air Inter was the last airline to use the Mercure of which only 12 were built. Phased out in 1995, the 162-seat twin-turbofan short-range airliner had started life in the early 1970s as an attempt to compete with the short-haul US twins. Over half of Dassault-Breguet's launch costs were funded by the French government but to no avail. Production ceased in 1975, the year that F-BTTI and BTTJ were delivered.

The Boeing 747SP was 48ft smaller than the standard 747-100, and designed to fly low-density routes at long ranges. It first flew on 4 July 1975 and looked as if it would be very successful, but only 50 were built.

OPPOSITE PAGE
ABOVE: EP-IAB, a 747SP-86 delivered to Iran Air (with which company it still flies) in 1976. Photo dated 1988.

BELOW and THIS PAGE ABOVE: SPJ6 B2442 delivered new to CAAC in February 1980.

CENTRE LEFT: N533PA was the fourth 747SP and, as with the first three, was delivered to Pan Am. This particular aircraft had been on a remarkable worldwide demonstration tour while under test, completing 75,150 miles in 29 days. Pan Am's SPs were taken over by United in 1986 when it bought Pan Am's Pacific Division.

BELOW LEFT: A 1977 view of one of the first of Iran Air's 747SPs, here EP-IAA.

The Cessna 404 Titan is a stretched Cessna 402B with a bigger tail and dihedral tailplane. There are two versions: the Titan Courier for freight (a large cargo door was an option); in its Titan Ambassador version it can carry up to 10 people including the pilot and is powered by two Continental GTS10-520-M turbosupercharged piston engines capable of c250mph at 20,000ft. It came out in 1976.

ABOVE: 3X-GCF of Aredor Guinee seen in 1987.

RIGHT: Air Westward's G-WTVC at Exeter in 1978.

The Swearingen/Fairchild Metro was developed by Swearingen from the Beech Queen Air. It first flew in 1979 since when it has sold a remarkable 900+ examples including 20 of the all-cargo Expediter variant. There is a military version – the C-26A which is used by the Air National Guard.

ABOVE LEFT: SA-226 Metro N27240 of Skywest.

ABOVE: SA-226 of Northwest Airlines seen in 1989.

LEFT: Another view of the same aircraft highlighting the tubular body and high nosewheel.

OPPOSITE PAGE: The unmistakeable lines of Concorde.

The Yak-40 (NATO code name 'Codling') first flew in 1971 carrying 24-32 passengers. The Yak-42 ('Clobber') was a scaled up version, which could carry 120 passengers.

RIGHT: Aeroflot Yak-42 CCCP-42644 at Le Bourget, 1991.

BELOW: Yugoslav Yak-40 at Farnborough, 1984.

BOTTOM: Another Yak-42 at Le Bourget: CCCP-42544 in 1985.

As these pictures show, there's nothing quite like the BAe/ Aérospatiale Concorde, the only supersonic transport aircraft in commercial service today. Operating since January 1976, the Concorde will still be flying into the next century. six French: (FBTSC/SD and F-BVFA/FB/FC/FF) and seven English: (G-BOAA/AB/AC/AD/AE/AF/ AG) are listed as still flying. With a max cruising speed of over Mach 2 at 51,000ft, a service ceiling of 60,000ft and a range of over 4,000 miles, the 1950s/60s technology has more than proved itself durable.

The Shorts SD3-30 – as the Shorts 330 was originally known – was based on the Skyvan, with an increased wingspan, stretched fuselage and retractable gear. Successful at home and abroad, an improved model was developed; originally designated 336, it became the 360. Production ceased in 1992 by which time 139 330s and 164 360s had been built. The 330/360 made an impact on the military scene, the US Air Force, Air National Guard and Army all using versions under the designation C-23 Sherpa.

THIS PAGE: Shorts SD330s – ABOVE: Guernsey's G-BITX in March 1987.

CENTRE and BELOW RIGHT: G-BEEO had a number of owners – here it is seen named Enterprise on British Airways' Royal Mail services in August 1987 and in Brown Air livery a year earlier.

OPPOSITE PAGE: Shorts SD360s – ABOVE: Capital's G-CPTL in May 1990.

BELOW: Gill Air's G-TBAC in October 1992. This company still uses Shorts 360s from its base at Newcastle airport.

Designed and built with the backing of the Canadian government, the DHC Dash 7 first flew in prototype form in 1975 and continued in production until 1988 when new owners Boeing decided to concentrate on the Dash 8. 114 aircraft had been built in three main versions – the 100 (freighter version 101), the 500 (freighter 501) and the IR Ranger which was an ice recce version for the Canadian government. Seating up to 50 passengers, the Dash 7 cruised at 266mph at its service ceiling of 21,000ft with a range of over 1,300 miles.

ABOVE: Dash 7 Demonstrator G-GNBX at Farnborough in 1986.

ABOVE RIGHT: Brymon Airways G-BRYA in December 1984. Brymon was an important West Country-based airline which contributed a great deal to the success of London City Airport in the early years. Today owned by British Airways, Brymon started using Dash 7s in 1982. Amongst its earliest acquisitions was Dash 7-100 G-BRYA which is still in service named Aberdeenshire.

RIGHT: Eurocity Express's G-BNDC, July 1987.

US Airports

As with British airports, those in the US have had to cope with increased traffic – but unlike their UK counterparts, the North American internal flights and distances are substantially greater than those in Europe and the flights greater in number.

OPPOSITE PAGE
ABOVE: Atlanta in March 1985.

BELOW: Chicago, Meigs Field, in July 1989.

THIS PAGE
ABOVE: Denver, Colorado in July 1989.

CENTRE LEFT: Miami in March 1988.

LEFT: New York JFK in February 1985.

The 1980s

The need for a smaller short-range Airbus became apparent in the 1970s and the Airbus 310 – at the time reported as the A300B10 – was the answer. The first version – the A310-100 – was not popular, but the A310-200 worked and by the end of 1996 261 examples of the A310 had been built.

RIGHT: A310-304 CS-TEH Bartolomeu Dias of TAP-Air Portugal seen in January 1990. CS-TEH is one of five 310-304s currently in service with Transportes Aeros Portugueses.

BELOW: KLM A310-203 PH-AGI Jan Toorop at Schipol in July 1985. The lowest altitude airport in the world – 10-15ft below sea level, built on land reclaimed from the sea in 1848-52 – Amsterdam's Schipol airport has been an extraordinary focus of aviation activity since 1919 when Albert Plesman formed the airline that would become KLM.

TOP RIGHT: A310-221 HB-IPC Schwyz of Swissair at Heathrow in 1984. Launch customer for the A310, Swissair is beginning to swap this aircraft for A321s.

BOTTOM RIGHT: Cyprus Airways' A310-203 5B-DAS Salamis in 1991. Formed in 1947, the company ordered A310s in 1984 and by 1996 its fleet was entirely composed of these or A320s.

OVERLEAF: A310-203 TC-JCU Sakarya of Turkish Airlines seen at Heathrow in October 1991. Today flying Airbuses, Boeing 727s and 737s, Turkish Airlines was formed by the Turkish government in 1933 and flew Dragon Rapides.

ABOVE and LEFT: The Ilyushin Il-86 succeeded the Il-62. Code-named 'Camber' by NATO, it was designed as a response to the 747: it could not meet Boeing's design parameters, seating a maximum of 350 and having engines which were distinctly poor relations to the turbofans of General Electrics or Pratt & Whitney. Only around 100 were built.

ABOVE RIGHT and RIGHT: The world's largest production aircraft when it first flew, the Antonov An-124 Ruslan is similar to the Lockheed C-5 Galaxy. It has a hinged nose, distinctive undercarriage, fly-by-wire control systems and is designed to operate in extreme conditions. Here examples are seen at Le Bourget (ABOVE RIGHT) and Farnborough (RIGHT) in the 1980s.

ABOVE: ATR42 F-GDXL is part of the Brit Air fleet based at Morlaix which undertakes Air France scheduled services. It is seen here in 1993. The ATR42 resulted from a union of Aeritalia and Aérospatiale to produce the Avion de Transport Régional with 42 seats. In service from late 1985 the ATR42 has proved very successful with over 250 produced for more than 50 airlines.

LEFT: The Beech 1900 commuter airliner (in the forground) seats up to 19 passengers and has proved very successful with commuter airlines in the USA. This is Interot's D-CISA in September 1990.

OPPOSITE PAGE
The Boeing 737-300 was a stretched, 128-seat improvement of the basic 737, incorporating new CFM International CFM56-3B engines.

ABOVE RIGHT: Southwest was the first customer to put the new model into revenue service in December 1984. Here N324SW is seen in July 1989.

CENTRE RIGHT: 737-300 G-PROC of Airways Cymru at Bristol in June 1986.

BELOW RIGHT: America West started services in 1983 from Phoenix, Arizona using 737-200s. Here N162AW, a 737-300 is seen in July 1989.

ABOVE: United Airlines was one of the early customers for the 737-200, at one stage – through secondhand purchases – reaching 70 examples of the type. 737-300s started reaching the company in November 1986 and numbers in service broke into three figures in 1990. Here a United 737 is seen in May 1993.

RIGHT: Iberia leased three 737-300s in 1988 for a short period of time. This photograph shows EC-EHX in April 1989.

BELOW: The first 737-300 to enter Lufthansa service joined its fleet of Series 200s in 1986. D-ABEA Saarbrücken is still flying with the airline, as are over 40 similar models. D-ABEA seen in October 1990. Behind it is D-AIPL Ludwigshafen am Rhein, an Airbus 320-211.

TOP LEFT: Boeing received Japan Air Lines' commitment to purchase 747-300s before it entered production. The first flight of the Series 300 was during 1982 and – until the 747-400 was announced – it proved popular with its improved drag characteristics, new P&W engines which improved power and fuel consumption.

Here 747-336 JA8178, still in service today, is seen in April 1989.

BOTTOM LEFT: UTA – Union de Transports Aeriens – received its first 747-300 immediately after the type got its passenger-carrying certificate in 1983. This example, F-GETA a 747-3B3 SCD, is today flying with Air France.

LEFT: Qantas is one of the world's oldest airlines, having been formed in 1920, and knows a good aircraft when it sees one! It was an early customer for the 737-300 series. VH-EBT City of Wagga Wagga is a 747-338 and is seen at Heathrow in November 1989 just over five years since its first flight on 6 October 1984.

ABOVE LEFT: Varig of Brazil is South America's largest carrier and it still flies 747-341 PP-VOA, seen here in January 1992.

BELOW LEFT: Singapore Airlines was formed in 1972 with the express intention to concentrate on international services. N119KE, delivered in 1984, was a 747-312, one of a sizeable order.

The MD-80 – originally designated the DC-9-60 – has three main versions, the MD-81, MD-82 and MD-83. The latter is capable of carrying 170 passengers.

RIGHT: Spanair's MD-83 EC-EOZ Sunbeam was delivered in 1989. The company was formed in March 1988 and flies mainly charters. Laid out with only tourist class seating, Spanair leased seven MD-83s.

BELOW: British Island Airways' MD-83 G-BNSB Island Equinox seen in April 1989. BIA started in 1982 based at Gatwick providing scheduled and charter services. Unfortunately it was forced out of business in 1990. G-BNSB was leased from International Lease Finance Corp from May 1988 until repossession in early 1990.

BELOW RIGHT: Airtours International was set up in 1991 with five leased MD-83s – one of which is seen here – later replaced by Airbus A320s.

The ATP – advanced turboprop – was BAe's successor to the Super 748, a regional airliner with space for 60-70 passengers. It did not prove hugely successful with sales only just over 50 despite being well supported by British Midland and British Airways. It first flew in 1986 and production ceased at Prestwick in mid-1994.

LEFT and ABOVE LEFT: G-MATP in the colours of United Express of Wisconsin, September 1992.

BELOW: British Midland Airways is based at East Midlands Airport, Castle Donington. This is G-BMYL.

BOTTOM: British Airways supported the ATP, buying 13. Today they are based in Glasgow, part of the Highland Division of BA Regional – which accounts for G-BTPC's name, Strathallan. The ATP is BA's only turboprop but, uniquely for a turboprop, it can use the terminal-linked boarding gates at most airports.

The Boeing 757 was designed as a replacement for Boeing's hugely successful 727 and is now used all over the world, with over 850 delivered or on order. These pictures show a range of users: British Airways (ABOVE LEFT), Britannia (BELOW LEFT), Delta Air Lines (TOP), Air Europe (ABOVE) and LTU Sud International Airways (LEFT) – the latter is a Munich-based German charter company.

The Boeing 767 and 757 twins were given a new lease of life when the FAA extended the limits of twin-jet operations under ETOPS – Extended Range Twin Operations – which permitted the use of suitable twin-engined airliners on long over-water routes. This led to the development of extended range (ER) versions of both aircraft. The 767-300ER can cruise at Mach 0.8 at its service ceiling of 40,000ft for a max range of nearly 7,000 miles. Over 700 767s have been ordered.

LEFT: US Air 767.

ABOVE: American Airlines N352AA, a 767-323ER, one of over 60 of the type in service with this major airline.

BELOW: 767-233ER C-GAVC of Air Canada.

The CASA 212 Aviocar is a successful twin turboprop commuter airliner which first flew in 1971. Over 500 have been sold, a good proportion of those built under licence by Nurtanio in Indonesia. The two companies have also collaborated on a C212 derivative, the CN235.

RIGHT: C212 N429CA of American Eagle in March 1986.

BELOW: Oceanair's N355CA.

OPPOSITE PAGE: Il-96-300 CCCP-96000 at Paris Le Bourget. The Ilyushin Il-96 is similar in appearance to the Il-76 but is in fact a completely new aircraft. Capable of carrying 300 passengers in its -300 version, and up to 375 in the P&W-engined Il-96M, the aircraft started full production in 1993. 12 Il-96-300s are in are in service with Aeroflot-Russia International which has orders for 20 of the M version.

Over 200 of British Aerospace's BAe146 were sold before production ceased in favour of the improved Avroliner. The 146 was notable for having an international construction – wings made in the US, tail in Sweden – and a remarkably low noise signature which allowed it access to city airports usually shunned by jets.

FAR LEFT: BAe146-200 G-CSJH of Air UK. Currently Air UK is the third largest scheduled airline in the UK.

BOTTOM LEFT: US Air BAe146 N173US seen in July 1989.

LEFT: BAe146-200 G-WAUS at North Weald in 1986.

BELOW: Loganair's G-OLCA, a BAe 146-200, at Guernsey. Loganair is still 'Scotland's Airline', serving the Scottish airports and islands with a range of smaller aircraft as part of British Regional Airlines.

RIGHT: Federal Express Cessna 208A Caravan 1 N827FE at Grand Junction in June 1989.

BELOW RIGHT: V2-LCV, a DHC Dash 8 of LIAT – the Caribbean Airline.

FAR RIGHT: Brymon is now a wholly owned subsidiary of British Airways. Before the takeover here is Dash 8 G-BRYG City of Bristol (which was named Lothian) in BA service.

BOTTOM: Lufthansa Cityline became a subsidiary of Lufthansa and received its name in 1992. Here is Dash 8 D-BEYT.

The Dash 8 was a follow-on to the Dash 7. A sleek twin-engined 36-seater it was launched in 1983 and entered service the following year. It offers a sparkling high speed cruise performance while still retaining some STOL characteristics. This combination has resulted in a substantial order book with almost 400 Dash 8s in service around the world at the end of 1996.

The Airbus 320 competed directly against the massively successful Boeing 737 and McDD MD-80, emphasising its operating cost reductions and new technology. Powered by two IAE V2500 or CFM56-5-A1 turbofans, the A320 can carry 150 passengers with a range of 2,930 miles. First deliveries were made to Air France in March 1988 and since then it has recorded no fewer than 787 orders up to August 1996.

ABOVE: Lufthansa D-AIPA Buxte Lude, a 320-211, in 1991.

RIGHT: Another Lufthansa Airbus A320-211: D-AIPE Kassel in 1990.

TOP RIGHT: Air France was the launch customer for the 320, taking the 320-111 version. This is F-GFKE Ville de Bonne in 1990.

FAR RIGHT: British Airways' A320-111 G-BUSB was originally ordered by British Caledonian and taken over by BA in 1988. It is the only member of the Airbus family to be sold to BA, which has preferred to date to buy mainly Boeing aircraft. The BA A320s are named after islands – G-BUSB is Isle of Jersey.

RIGHT and BELOW: The Canadair Regional Jet stemmed from a proposal for a stretched CL610 Challenger. When Bombardier bought Canadair, the money to develop the project was secured and it flew first in 1981. Bombardier was also able to take away one of the competitors to the Regional Jet when it bought Shorts in 1989, putting paid to that company's RJX. Lufthansa Cityline was the Regional Jet's launch customer, with Lauda Air being the first to receive the 100ER version whose range was extended to over 1,800 miles. This one of Cityline's 100ERs seen in June 1993.

ABOVE: Dornier Do228-200 of Delta Air at Farnborough in 1984. A successful twin-turboprop commuter airliner, the Do228 was built under licence by Hindustan Aeronautics as well as in Germany. About 250 have been produced in total. Delta Air – now known as Deutsche BA – is 49 percent owned by British Airways following purchase in 1993 and no longer flies Do228s.

The EMBRAER EMB-120 Brasilia first flew in 1983 and has proved a highly popular design. Over 500 of this twin-turboprop regional airliner have sold. Launch customer was Atlantic Southeast Airlines of the USA; DLT – now Lufthansa Cityline – took the first in Europe.

CENTRE LEFT: United Express EMB-120RT N280UE in July 1989.

BELOW LEFT: Comair EMB-120 in July 1991.

The MD-11 was a derivative of the DC-10 with a lengthened fuselage seating up to 405 passengers, combined with a revised wing design, other aerodynamic refinements, an advanced two-crew flightdeck and new generation high thrust turbofans. The standard MD-11 is capable of carrying a full payload over 6,900 miles while the MD-11ER can carry 298 passengers over a staggering 8,300 miles. The aircraft is also produced in freighter and combi versions. Sales have been slow, with only 174 ordered to the end of 1996.

Swissair has a number of MD-11s; illustrated are HB-IWA Obwalden (ABOVE), HB-IWE Nidwalden (RIGHT), HB-IWC Schaffhausen (TOP RIGHT) and HB-IWB Graubünden (BOTTOM RIGHT).

BELOW: Brazilian carrier Varig's PP-VPK.

The Boeing 737-400 first flew in 1988. A stretched 737-300 (it's 10ft longer) it can accommodate 169 passengers. Piedmont was the first airline to order it, Air UK Leisure the first European carrier to receive it.

OPPOSITE PAGE ABOVE LEFT: British Airways ordered 25 737-436s at a crucial time for the airliner. In the face of severe competition from Airbus, BA stood by its decision to buy Boeing and the first 737-436, delivered in October 1991, was the 1000th 737 produced. Later BA took over nine ex-Dan Air aircraft when it acquired the company. These aircraft were 737-4Q8s and are based at Gatwick.

BOTTOM LEFT: Air Europe 747-400 at Gatwick.

ABOVE: Aer Lingus 737-448 EI-BXD St Colman in April 1991.

CENTRE LEFT: Piedmont N405US in July 1989.

LEFT: Air Europe G-BPKB in August 1990.

Saab-Scania and Fairchild Industries collaborated in producing the SF340, a twin turboprop regional airliner which has sold well to US airlines. Fairchild pulled out in 1985 but the aircraft has gone on to sell over 350 examples. Illustrated are 340A F-GELG of Brit Air, flying in Air France livery (RIGHT) and a Northwest Airlink 340 (BELOW).

OPPOSITE PAGE: The Fokker 50 is derived from the Fokker F27-500 with twin P&W Canada PW125B turboprops and distinctive six-bladed propellers. Illustrated are 9M-MGA of Malaysian Airlines (ABOVE) and Air Lingus's EI-FKB (BELOW) named St Fergal. Over 170 Fokker 50s are in service but production has ended following the collapse of the company in 1996.

European Airports

European airports have flourished in the last decades of the 20th century. This selection shows some of the better-known.

ABOVE: Amsterdam's Schipol has been a cradle of aviation from the very earliest years.

CENTRE RIGHT: A TWA TriStar is seen at Brussels National airport at Zaventem.

BELOW RIGHT: Düsseldorf's B pier has the apron control tower on its roof. Here an SAS DC-9.

OPPOSITE PAGE
ABOVE: Work started on Paris Charles de Gaullle in 1966 but, as with so many things to do with air travel, the anticipated growth of business was not estimated correctly and it had reached saturation point by the 1970s, A second terminal was opened in 1982.

BELOW: Faro airport in Portugal is not as big as many in Europe, but is destination of many holidaymakers.

The 1990s

TOP: Japan Airlines is the world's biggest operator of 747s. Here 747-446 JA8081.

RIGHT: BA's 747-436 G-BNLR City of Hull.

BELOW RIGHT: A subsidiary created in 1993 to fly to Taiwan, British Asia Airways' only aircraft is 747-436 G-BNLZ City of Perth.

FAR RIGHT: BA's 747-436 G-BNLA City of London. British Airways initially ordered 16 747-400s, the number in service rising to 37 by end 1996.

OVERLEAF: British Airways' G-BNLJ City of Nottingham, a 747-436.

ABOVE: NFD ATR72 D-ANFF. In 1992 NFD merged with RFG to become the Nuremberg-based Eurowings. It has 11 ATR72s with more on order.

RIGHT: American Eagle is American Airlines' commuter line. The ATR72-210 saw a massive 60-aircraft order from American. A substantial stretch of the ATR42, the 72 can carry over 70 passengers.

BELOW RIGHT: The Dornier Do328 twin turboprop regional airliner entered service in North America with Horizon in November 1993.

OPPOSITE PAGE
ABOVE: EMBRAER CA-123 Vector PT-ZVE at Farnborough in 1990.

BELOW: The Saab 2000 first flew in 1992. A twin turboprop regional airliner, launch customers were Crossair and Deutsche BA. This is the demonstrator at Farnborough in September 1992.

When Boeing launched its 757 and 767 it was seen as direct challenge to the Airbus consortium. Airbus also went ahead with a pair of complementary designs which became the wide-bodied A330 and A340. In some respects these were actually the same aircraft as they had identical fuselages and similar wing structures, the most obvious difference being the powerplants.

The A330 was a twin-jet, intended for high capacity medium to long range routes, and at the time of its maiden flight, the A330 was the largest twin-jet airliner to have flown. The A330 flew almost a year behind the A340, in November 1992, and the initial production variant was the long fuselage A330-300 which typically seated 335 passengers in two classes or 295 in a three-class layout. This prototype was powered by two General Electric CF6-80 turbofans but production aircraft were offered with Pratt & Whitney PW4000s or Rolls-Royce RB211 Trents, the first time that the British manufacturer had succeeded in hanging one of its engines on an Airbus wing. The 330 entered service with Aer Lingus, Air Inter and Thai Air.

The A340 was a four-engined aircraft with emphasis on ultra long range. It took to the air in October 1991 and was subsequently produced in two versions, the A340-200, seating around 263 passengers and the A340-300 with a lengthened fuselage carrying 295 passengers. These entered service with Lufthansa and Air Inter respectively early in 1993. Optimised for very long range flights, the -200 can carry its payload over a range of 7,200 miles while the larger A340-300 can reach out to 7,300 miles.

ABOVE: Singapore Airlines took delivery of its first A340-300 in April 1996.

RIGHT: Virgin's G-VBUS Lady in Red, an A340-311.

BELOW: Currently under development is the A340-600 which will seat 375 passengers.

LEFT: Lufthansa was the launch customer for the Airbus A321 – the stretched A320. It was also an early purchaser of the A319 which was launched at the 1992 Farnborough Air Show. Currently Lufthansa has 11 A319s, here A319-114 D-AILA Frankfurt.

ABOVE: Airbus A319 in United Airlines' livery.

BELOW: Swissair has eight A321s which will take over from its A310s and Fokker 100s. Here A321-111 HB-IOA Lausanne.

OVERLEAF: The McDonnell Douglas MD-90 first flew in 1993. Powered by International Aero Engines V2500 turbofans it is designed to carry about 150 passengers. A total of 143 MD-90s had been ordered by the end of 1996.

All Nippon Airways was one of Boeing's initial partners working together to produce the 777. ANA became the first airline in the Asia-Pacific region to take delivery of the new twin-jet in October 1995. It has ordered 28 777s — one of 20 airlines worldwide to order Boeing's new wide-bodied jetliner. There is little doubt that Boeing will end the century as the leading manufacturer of jet airliners, with few major airlines running a fleet without a Boeing aircraft in its inventory.

Civil aviation has come a long way from the early post-WW1 days. The Boeing 777 involved a test programme of almost 7,000 flying hours. It can carry over 400 passengers, powered by the most powerful engines fitted to a civil airliner. Its ultra long range version will be capable of ranges in excess of 9,200 miles — a far cry indeed from AT&T's DH4A.